Color & Enjoy !

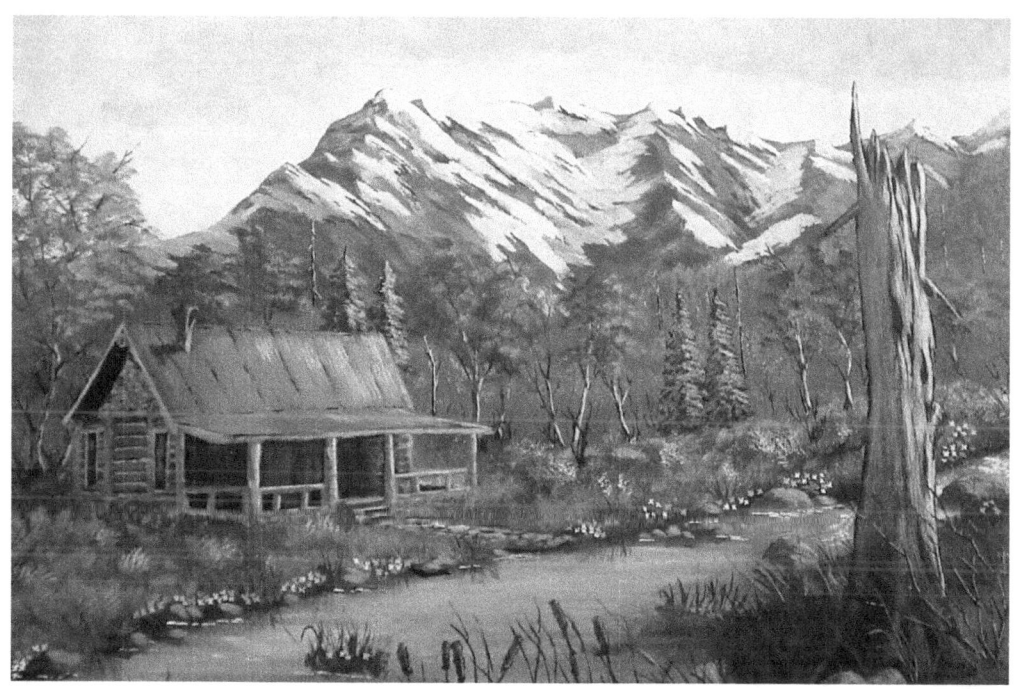

Landscape & Outdoors Coloring Book
Volume 1

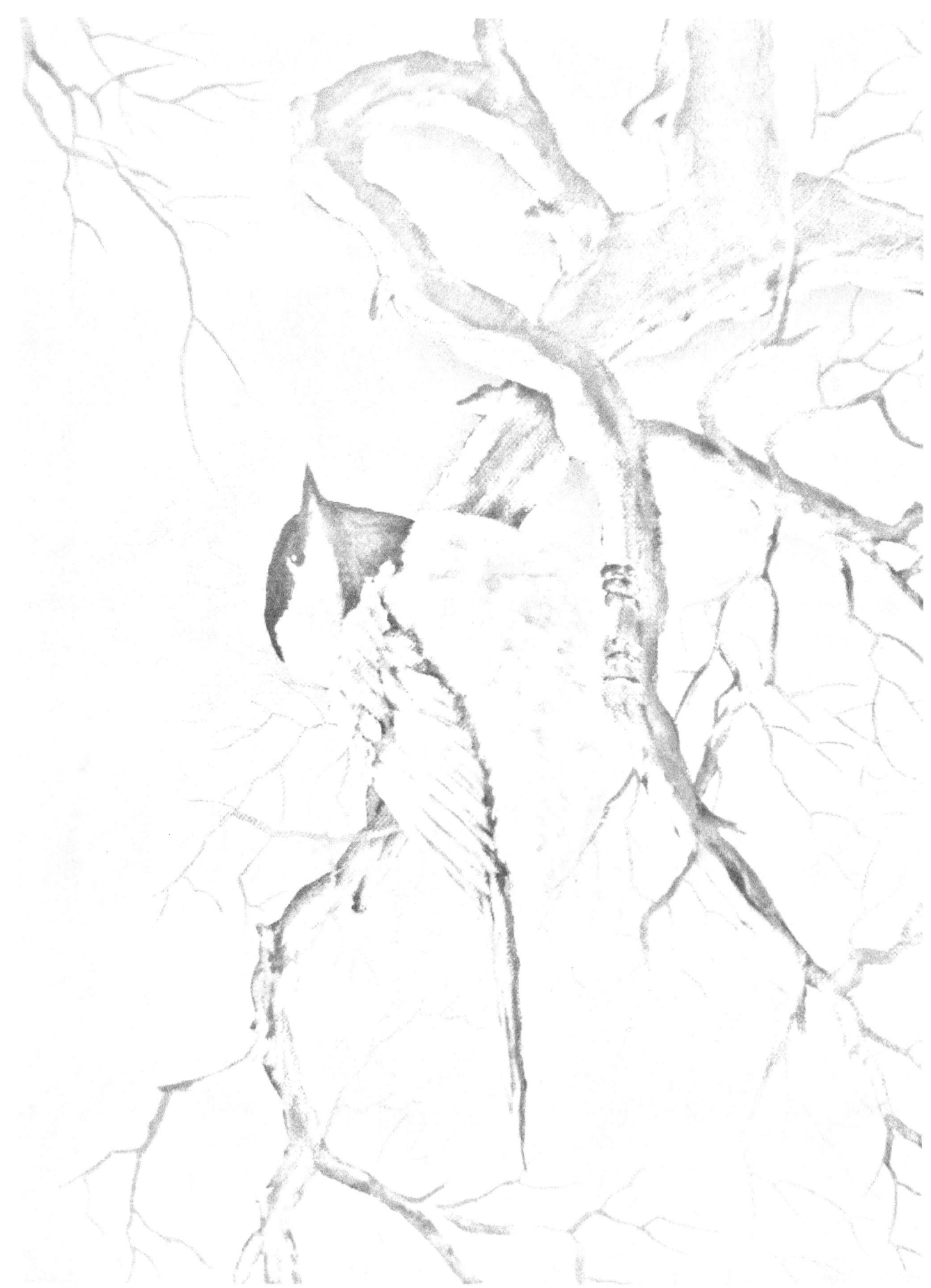

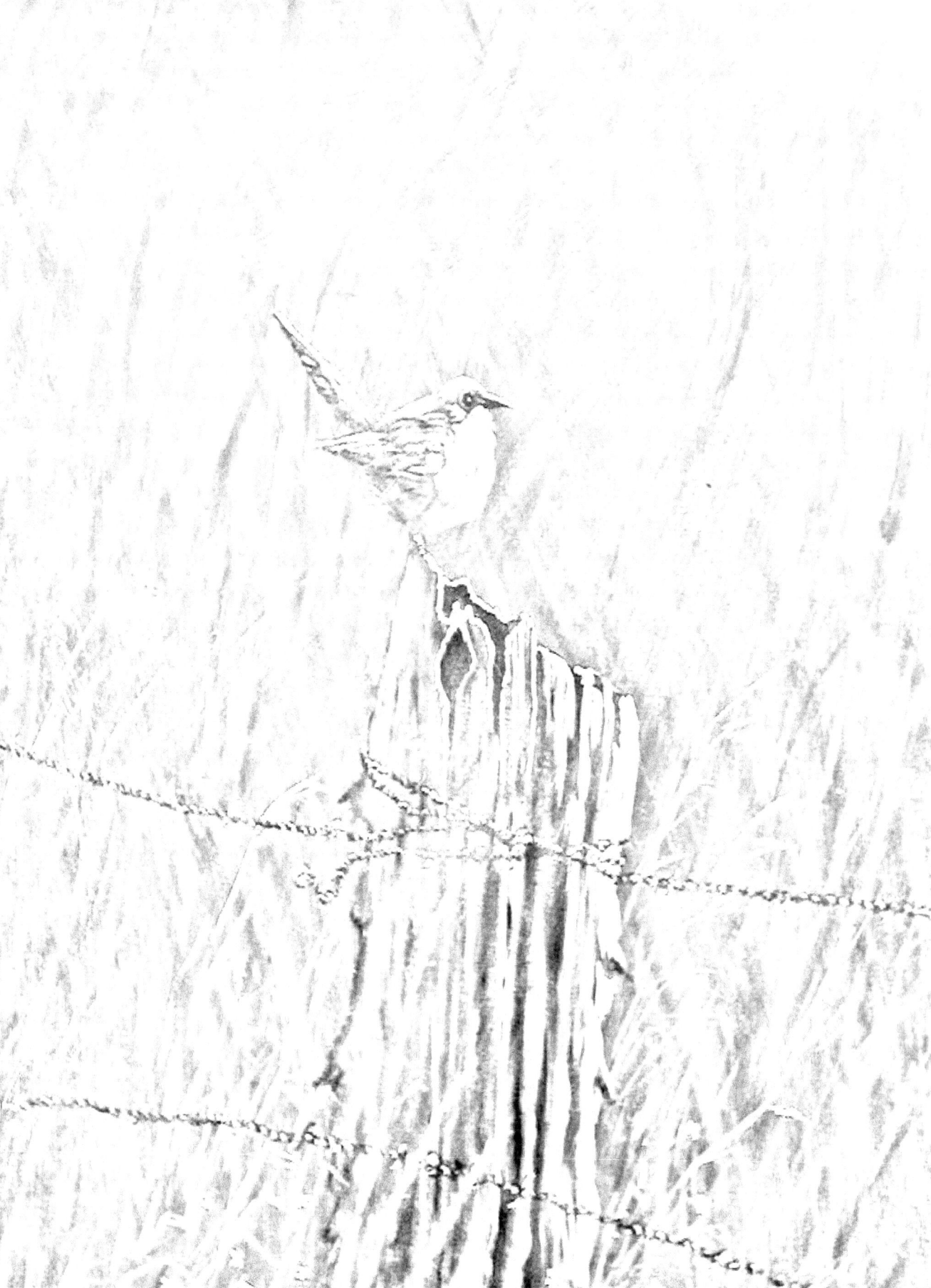

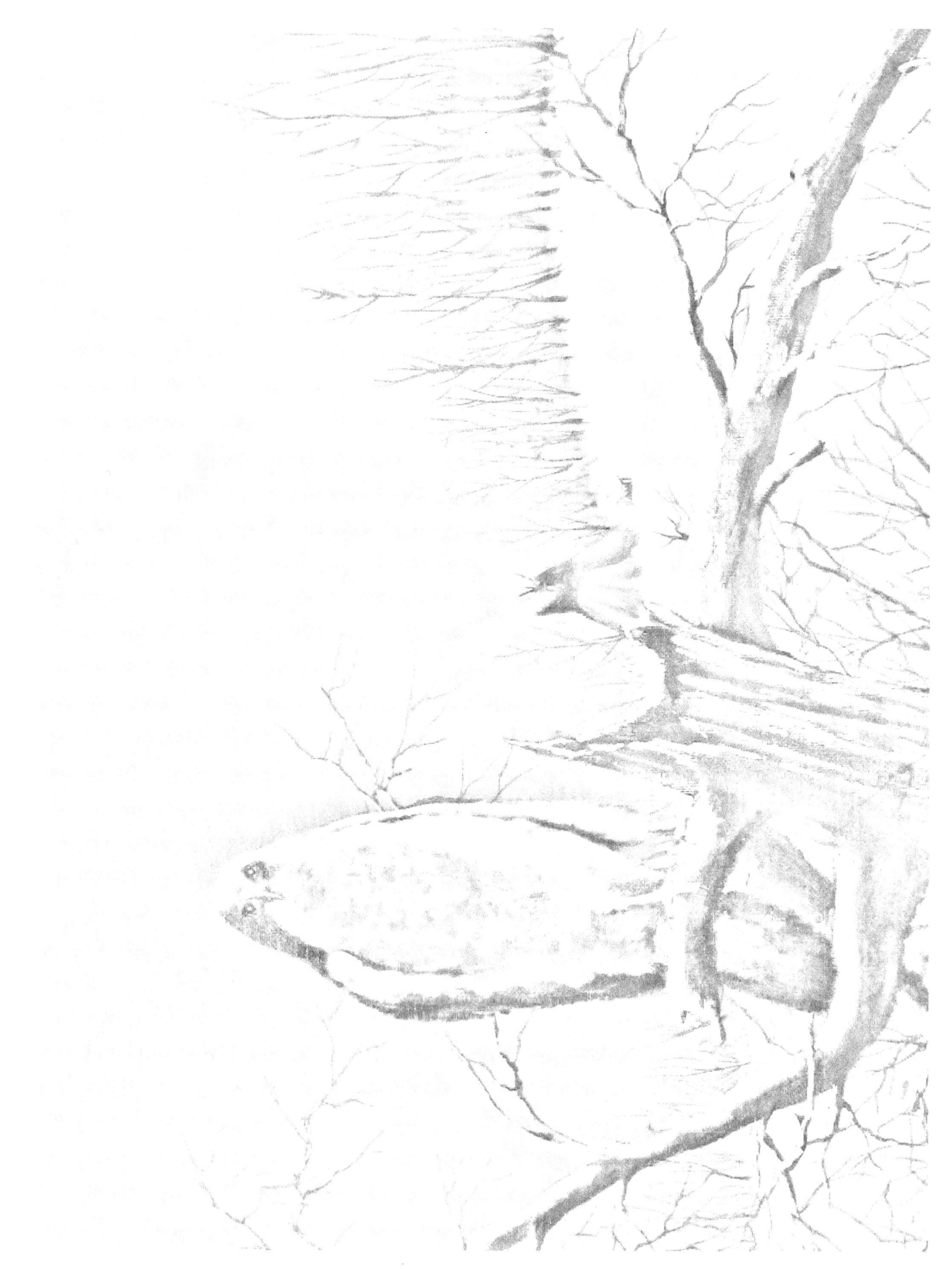

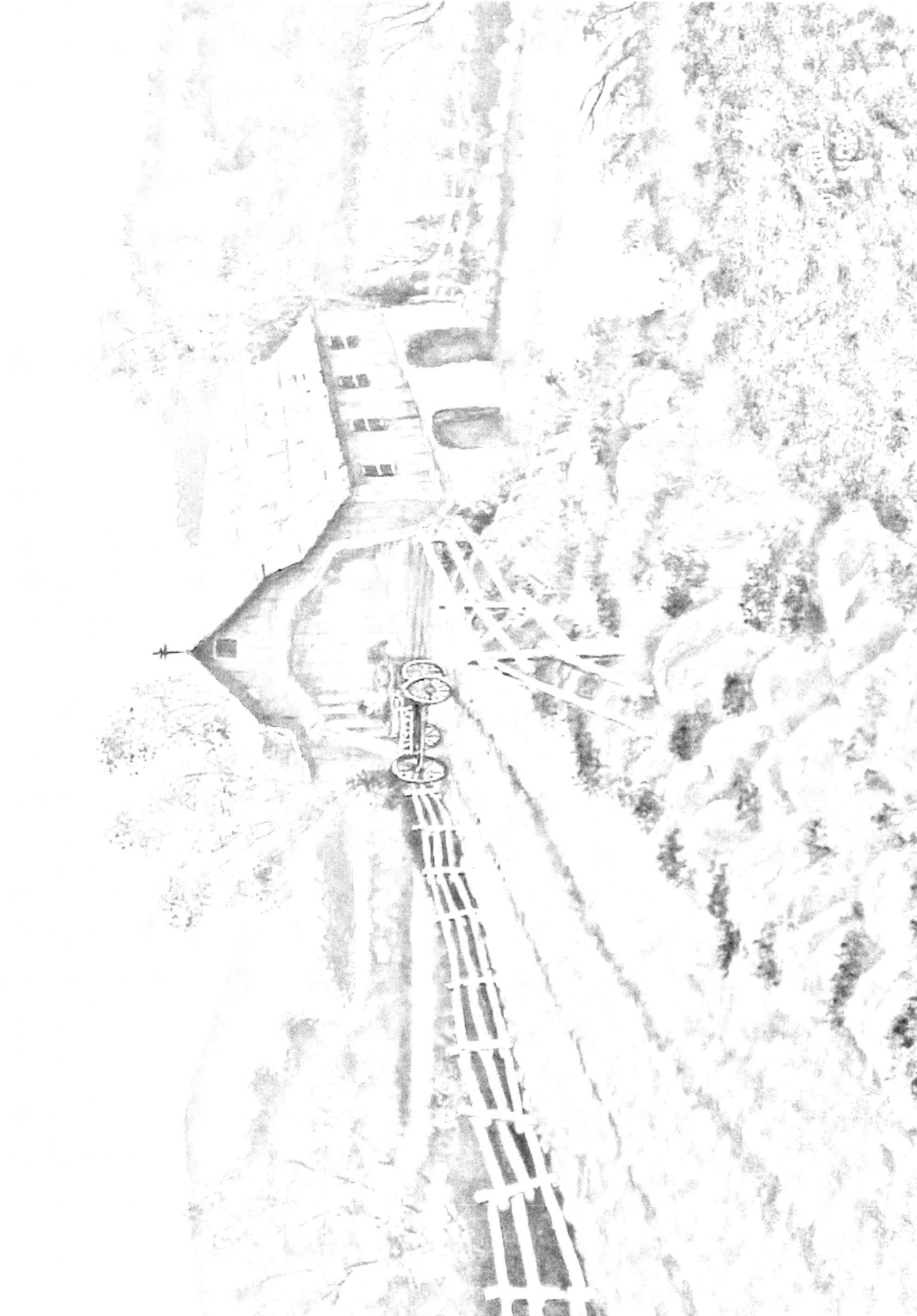

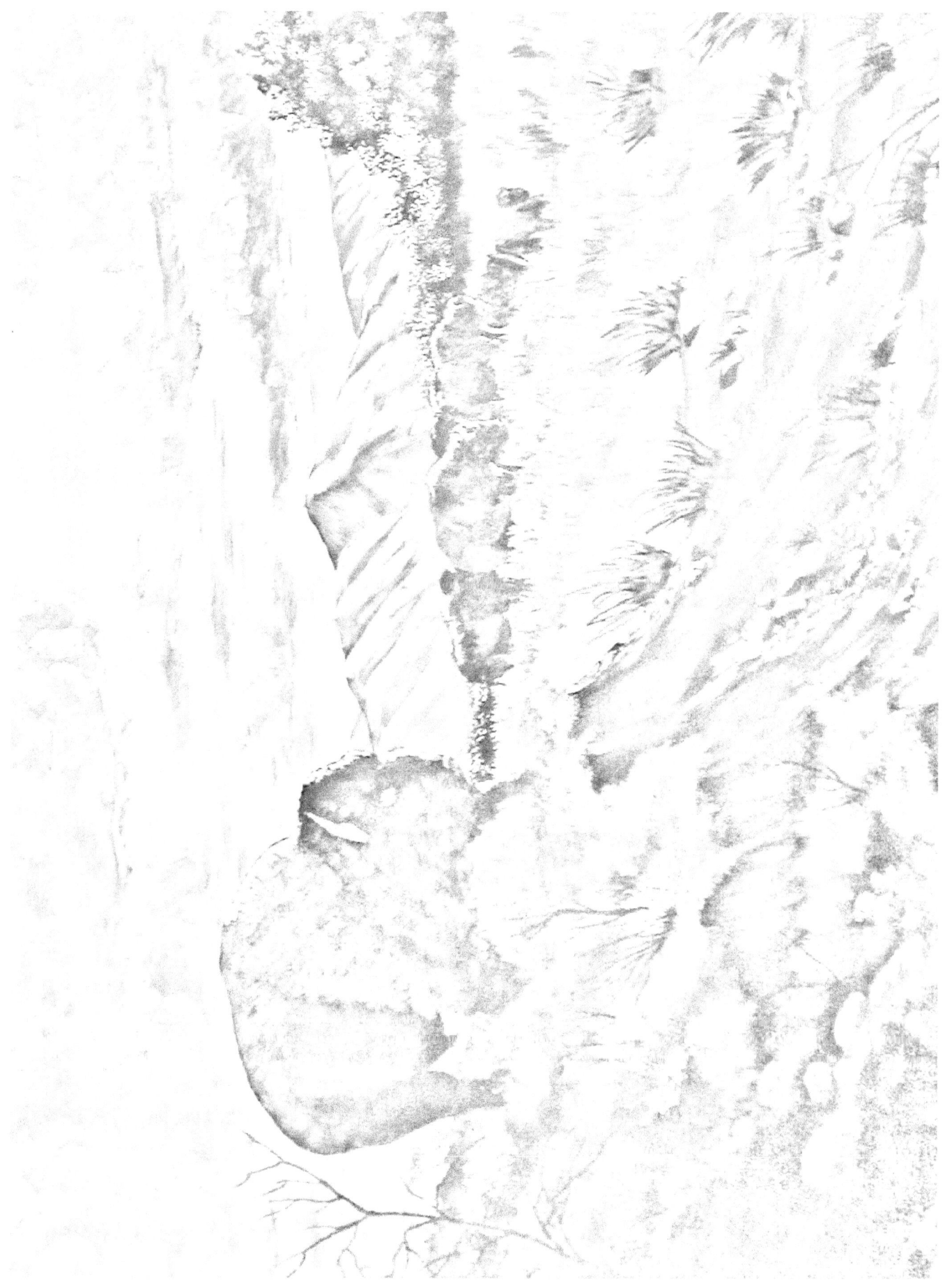

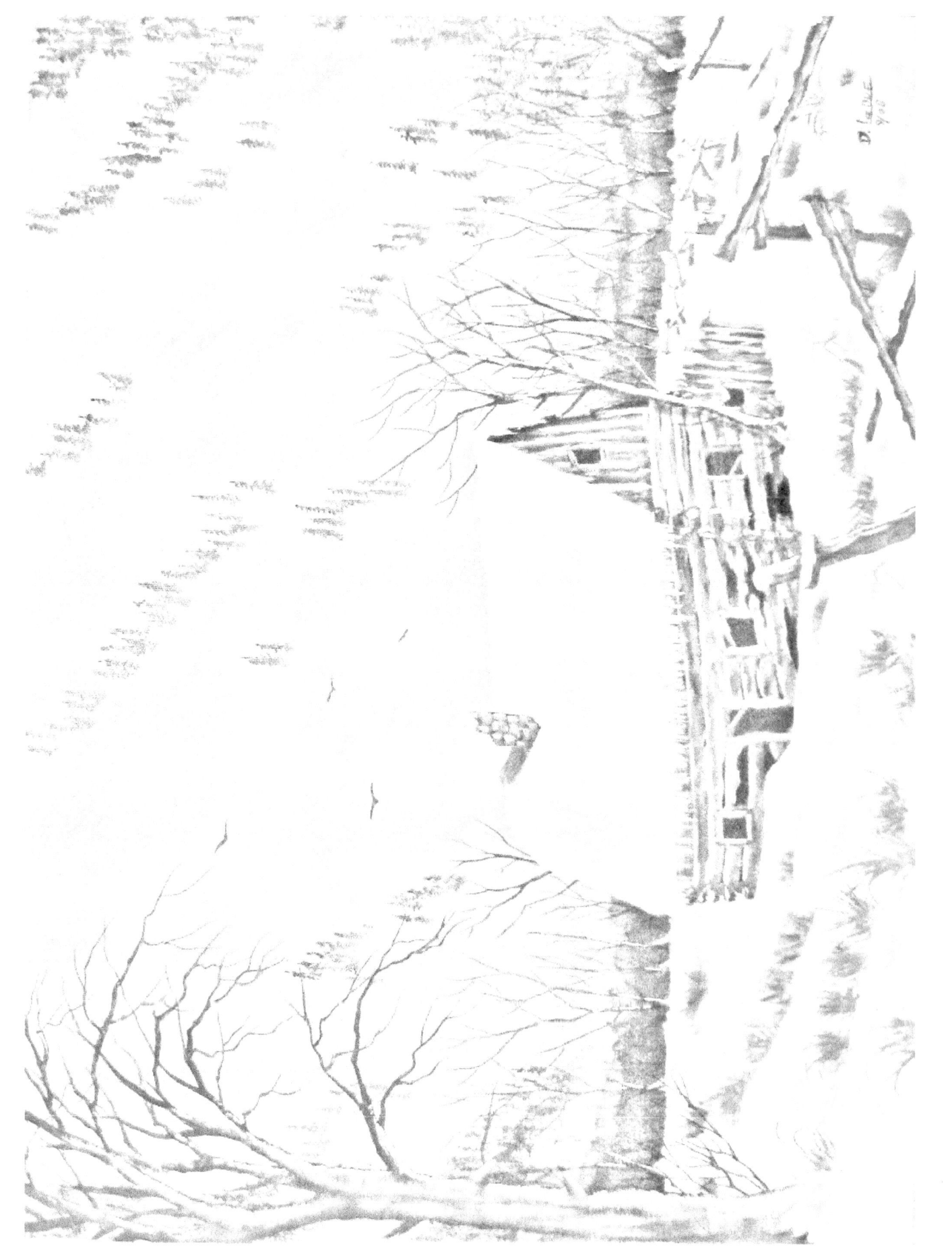

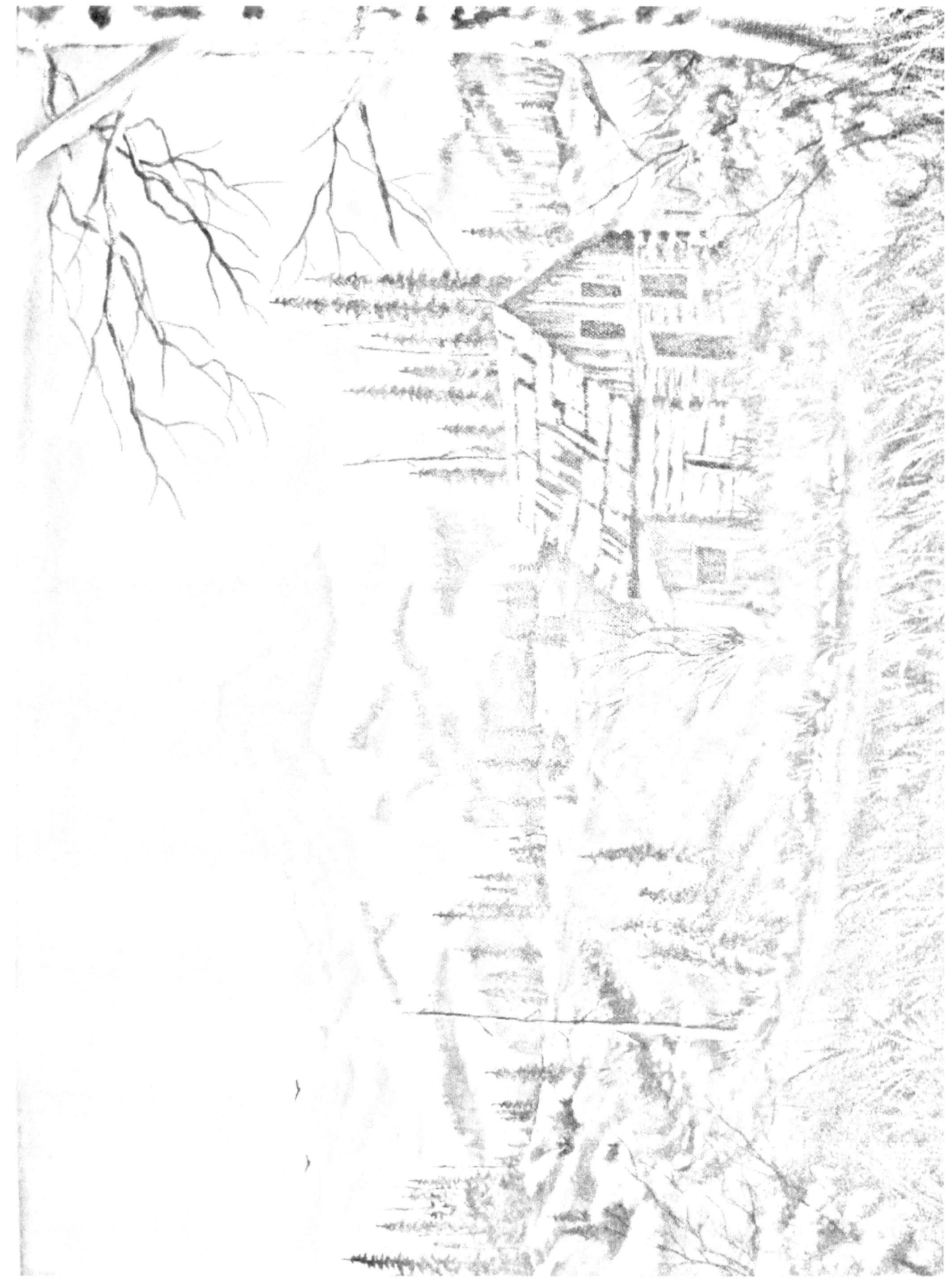

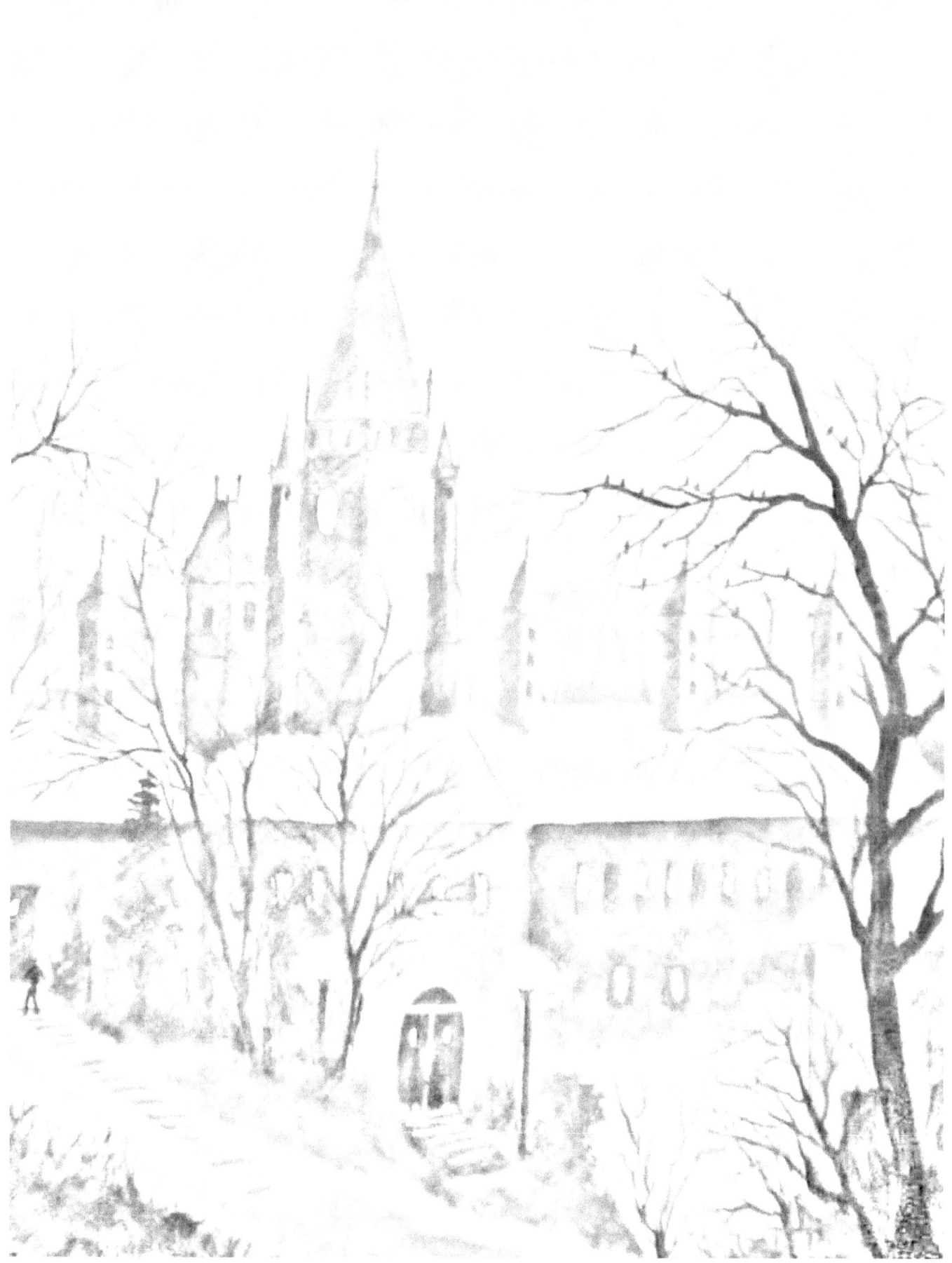

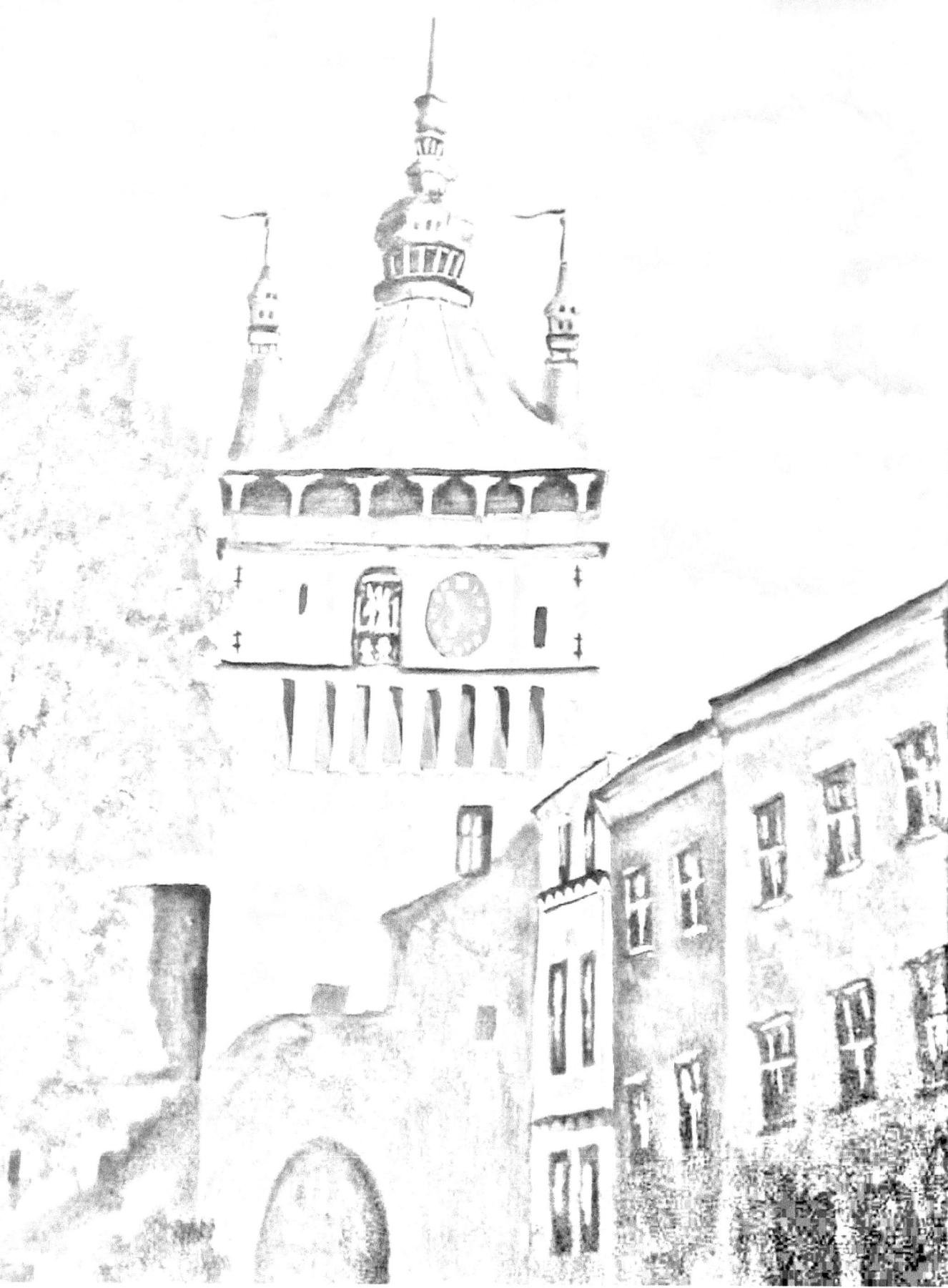

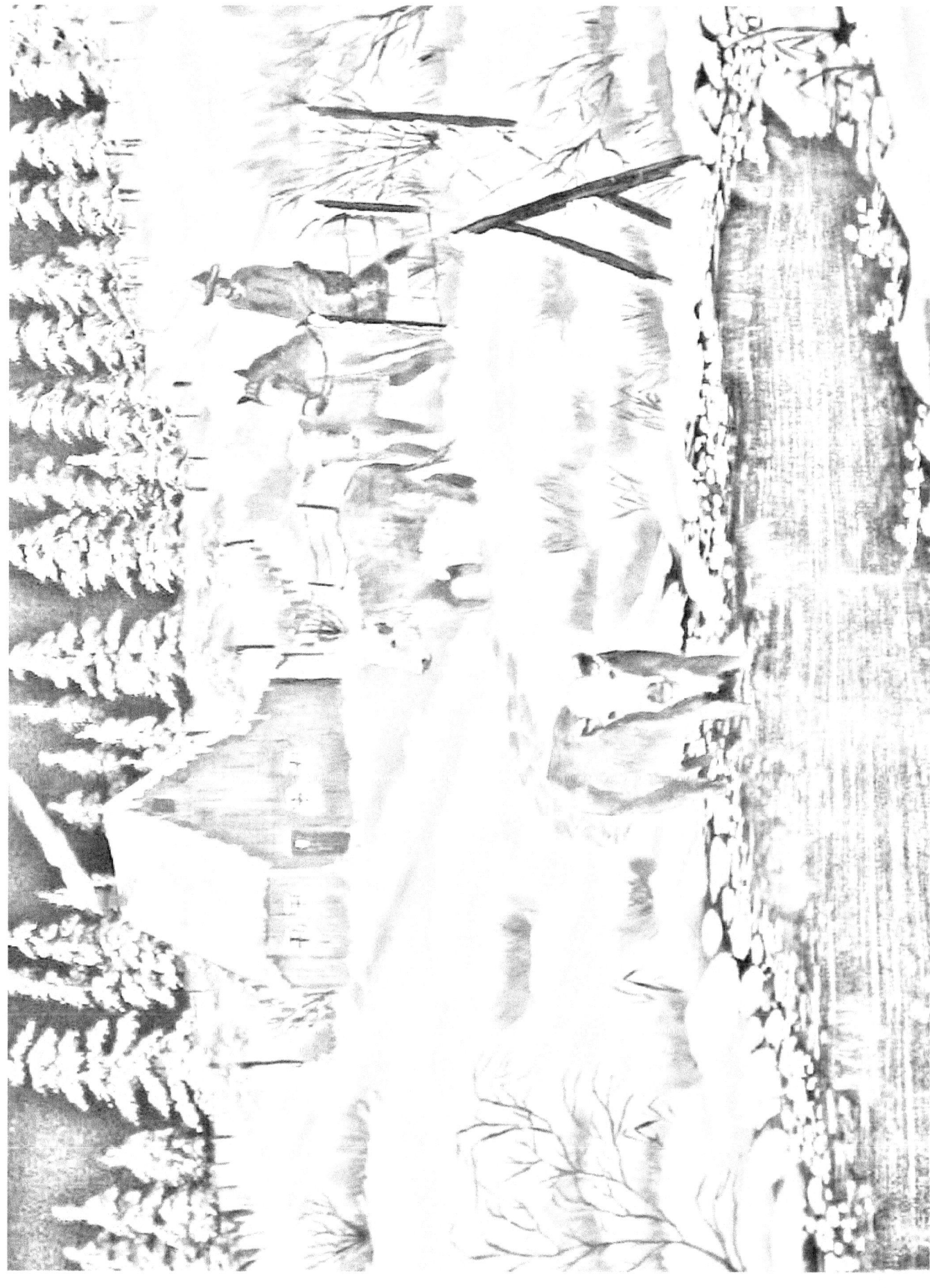

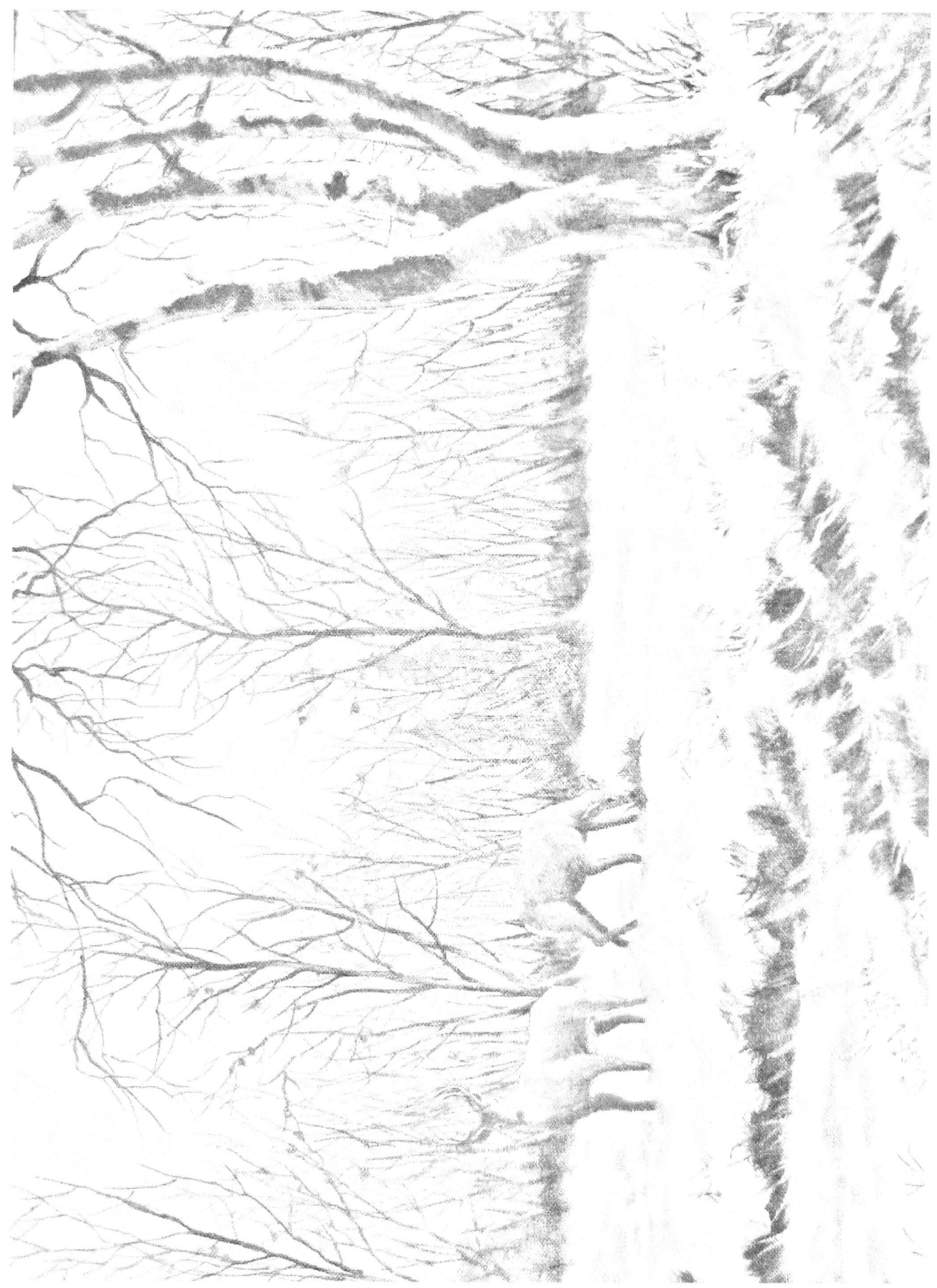

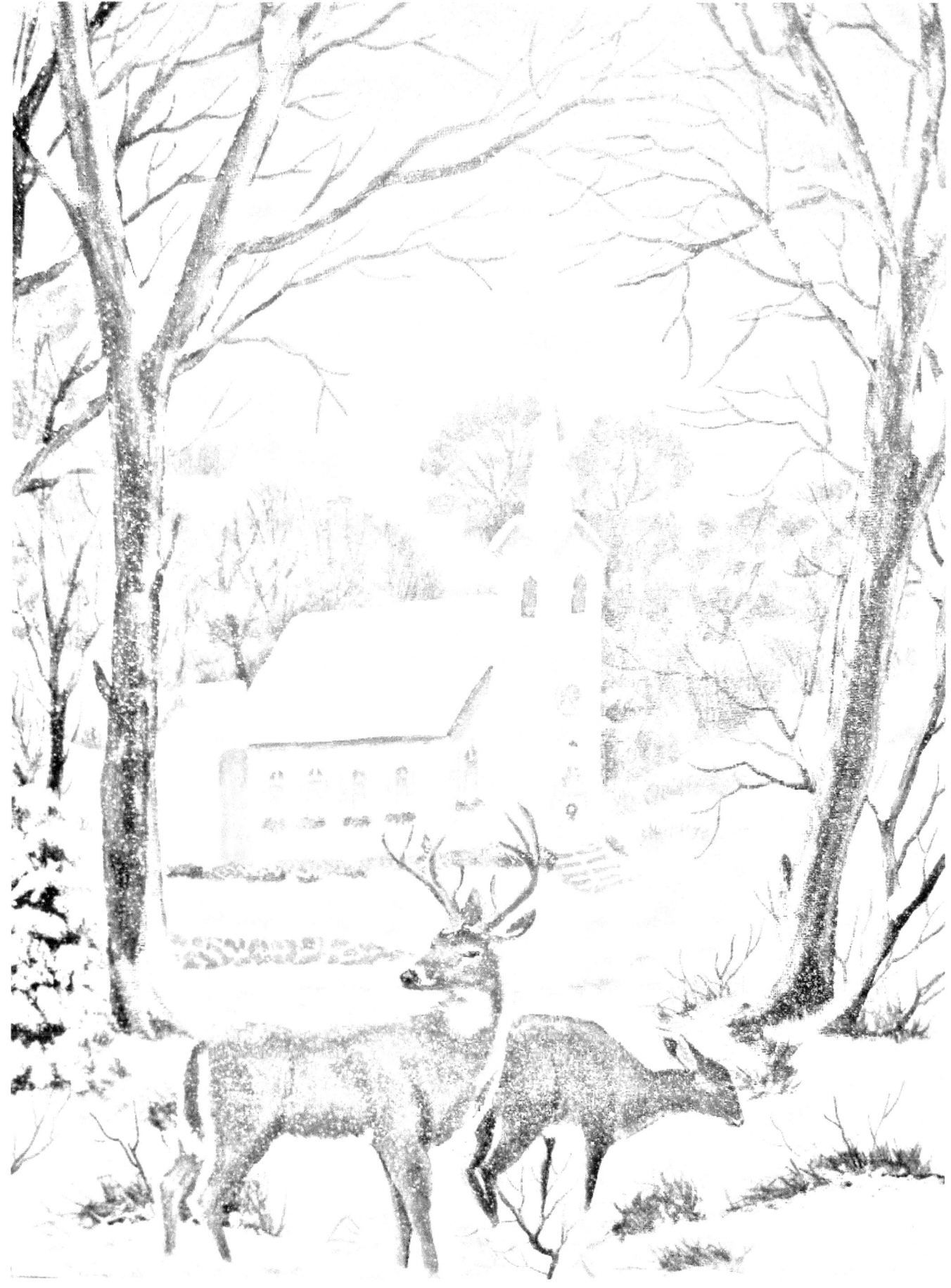

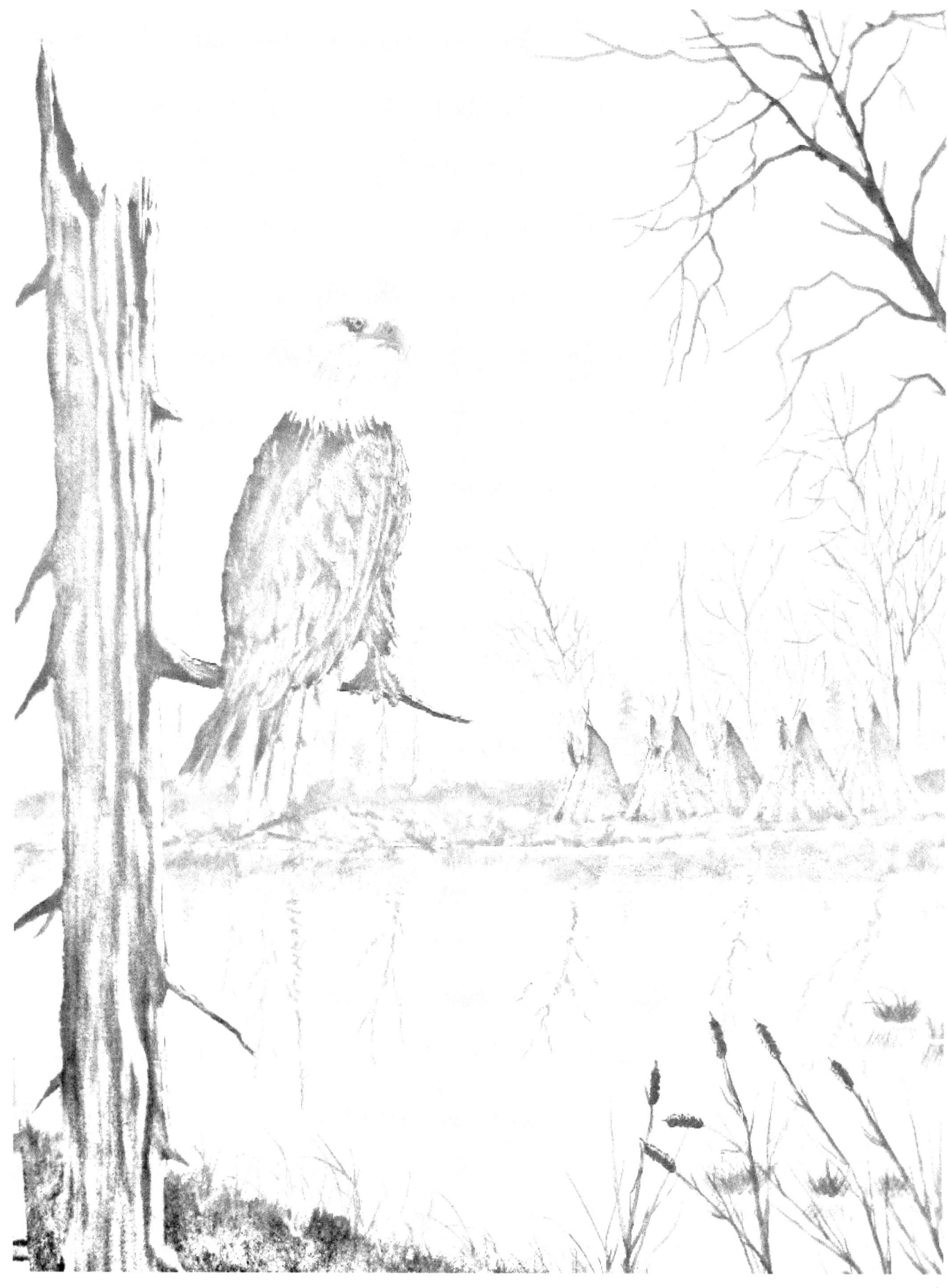

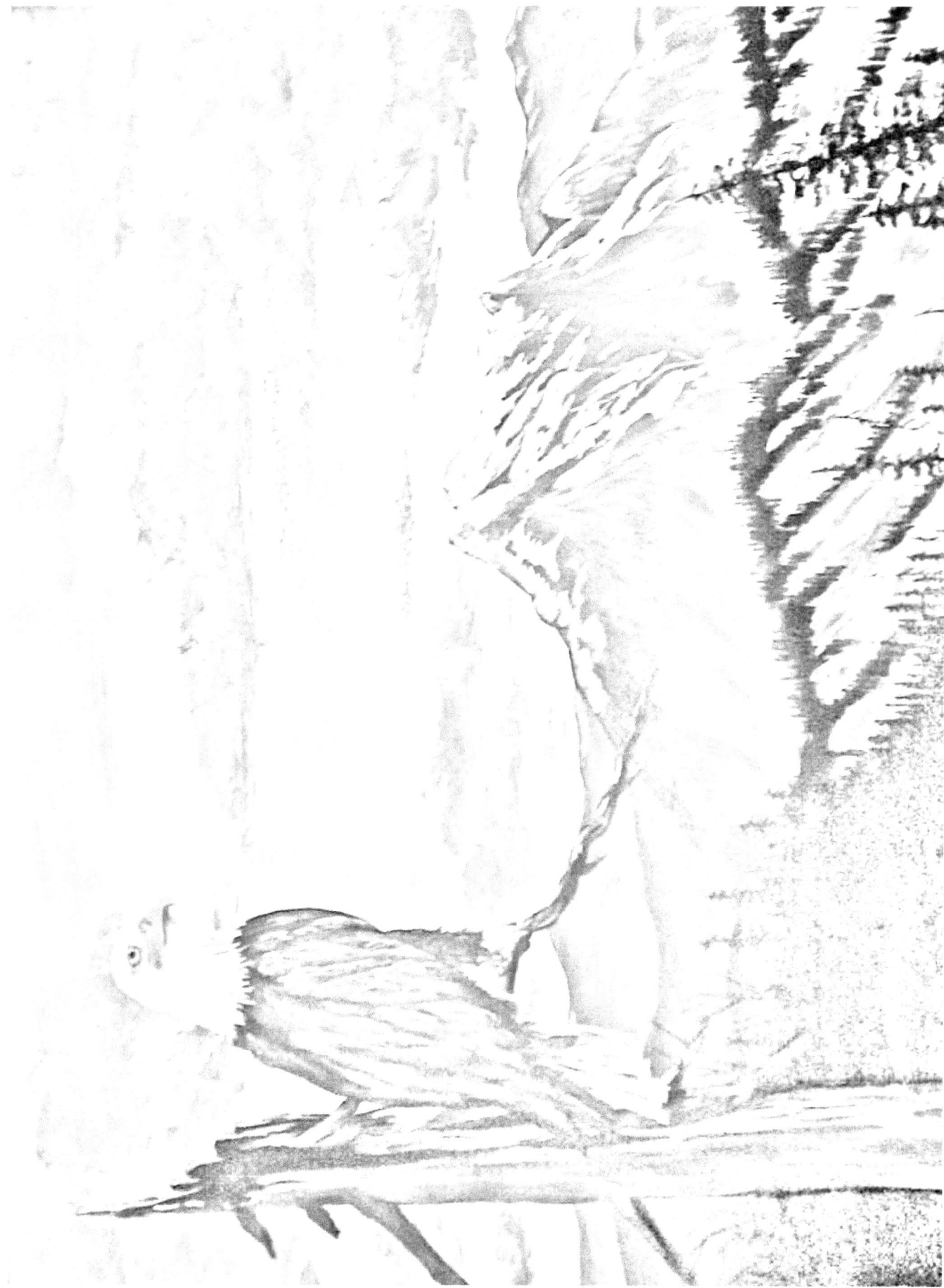

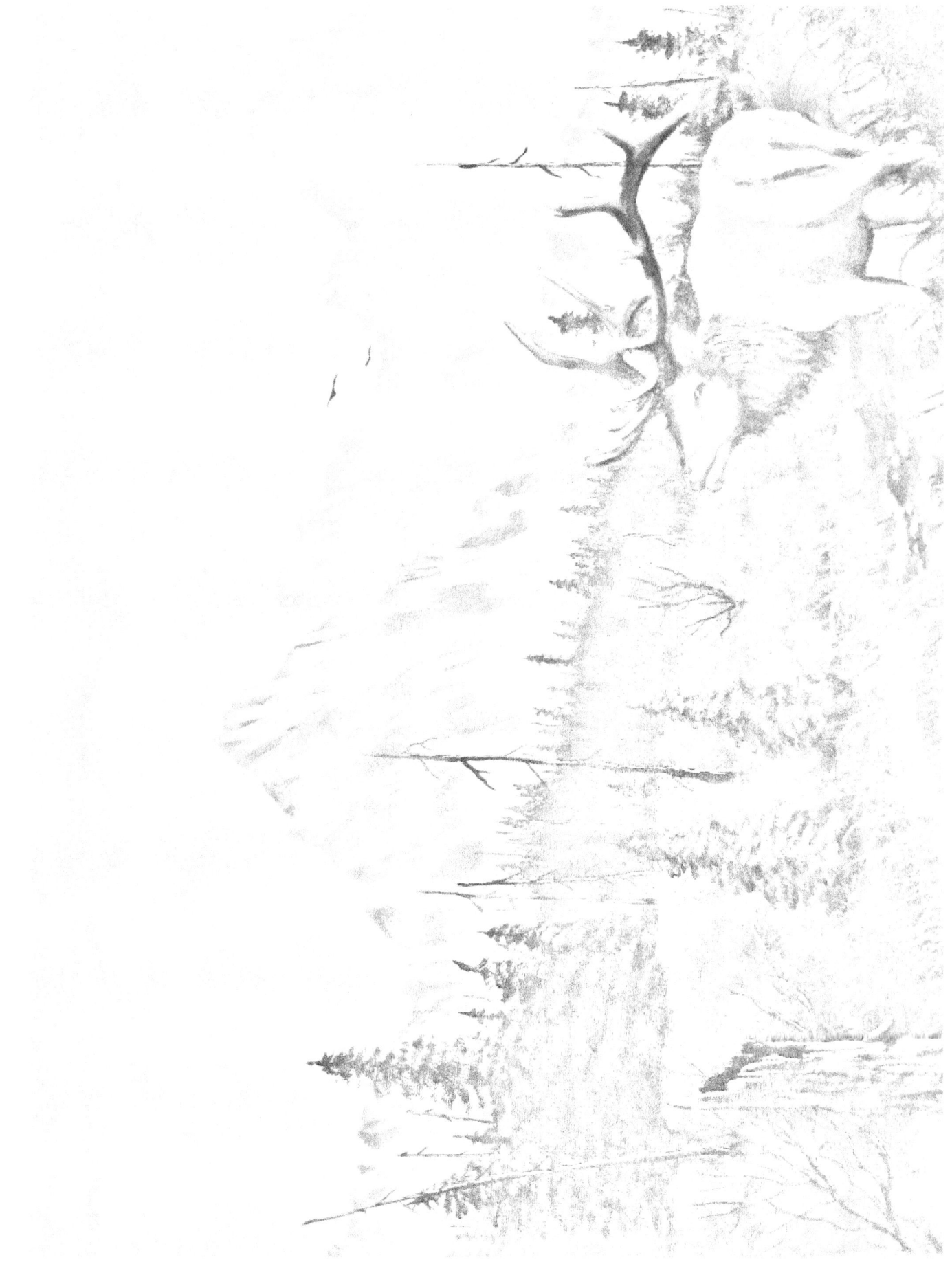

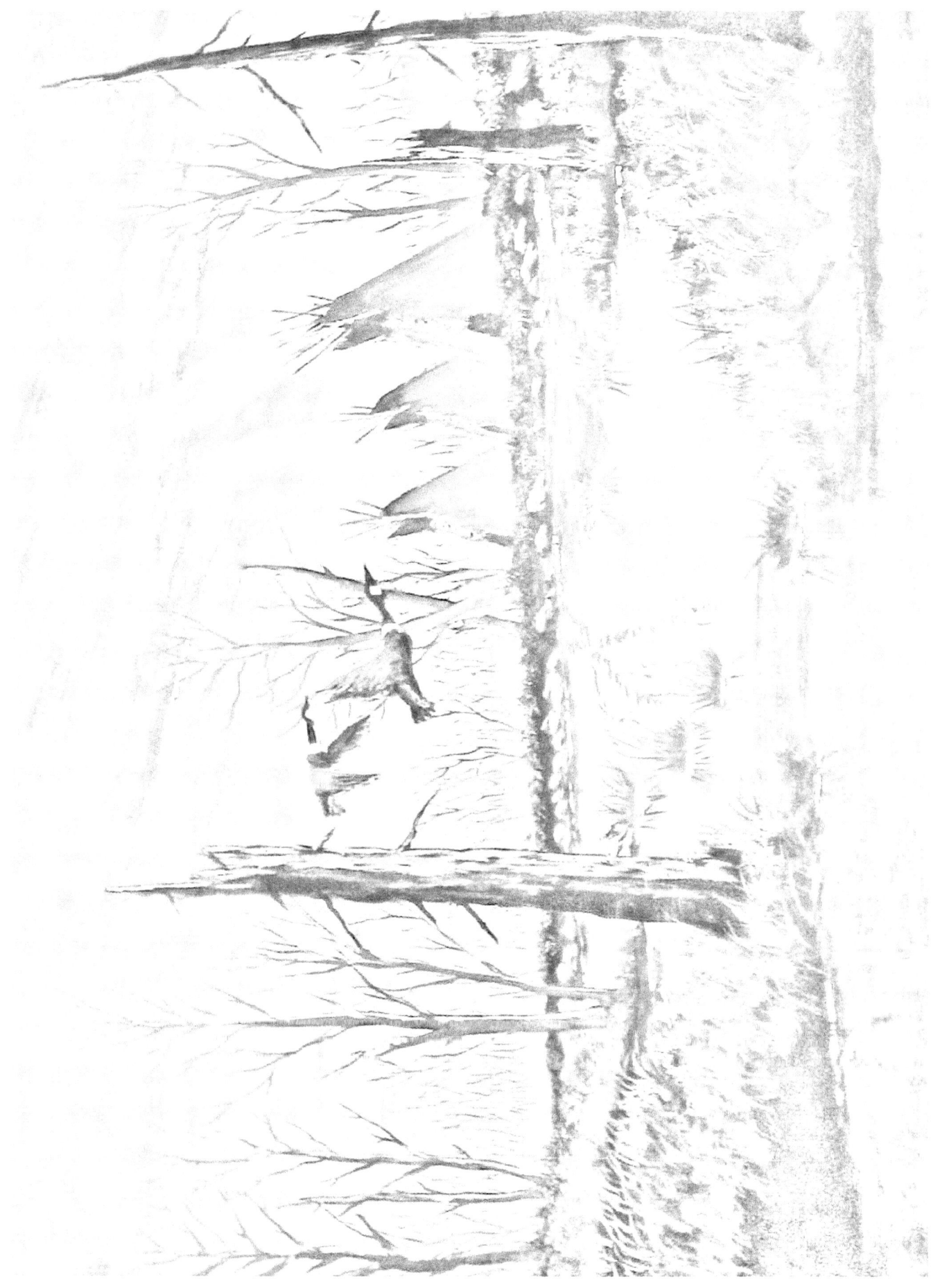

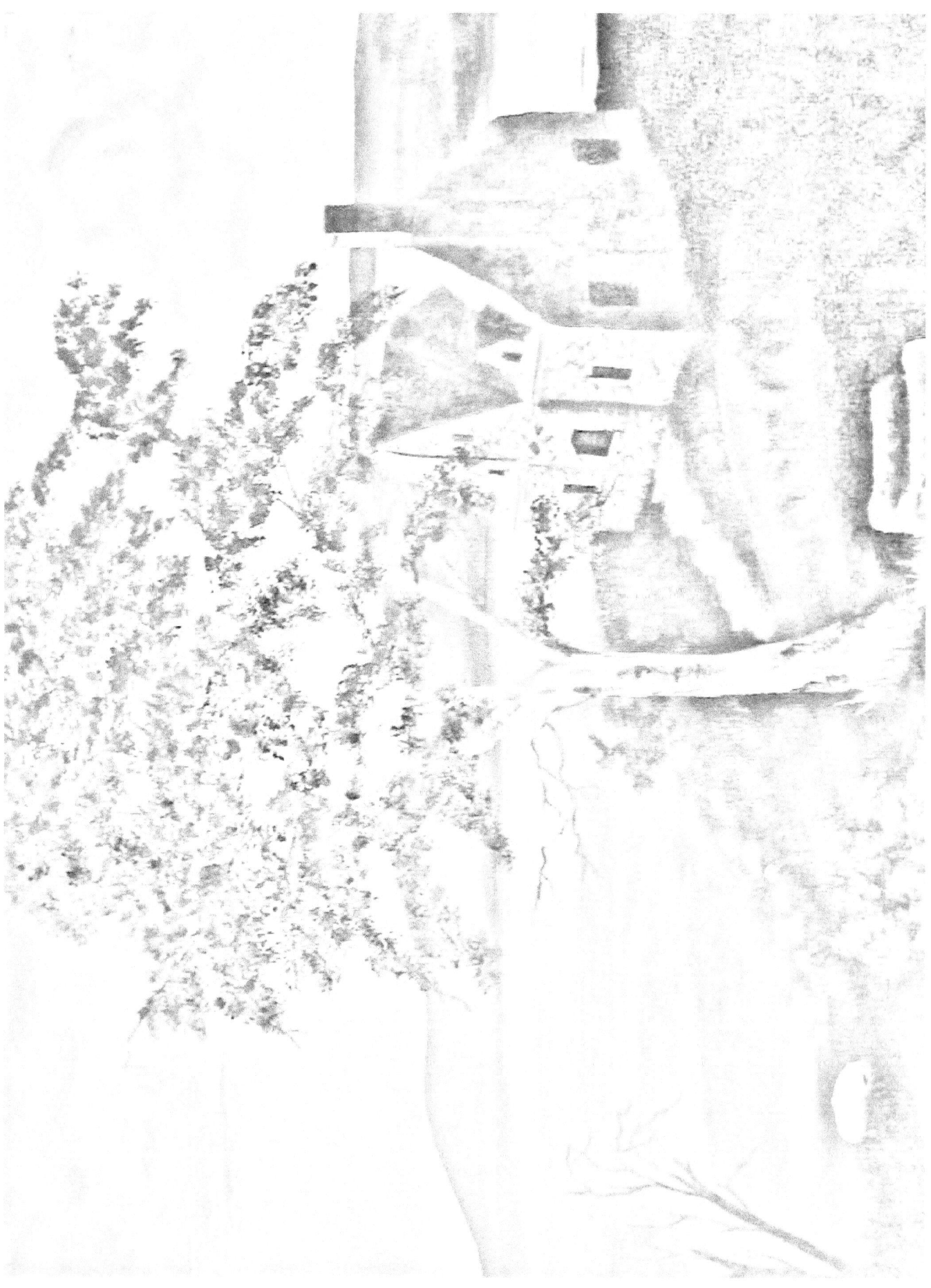

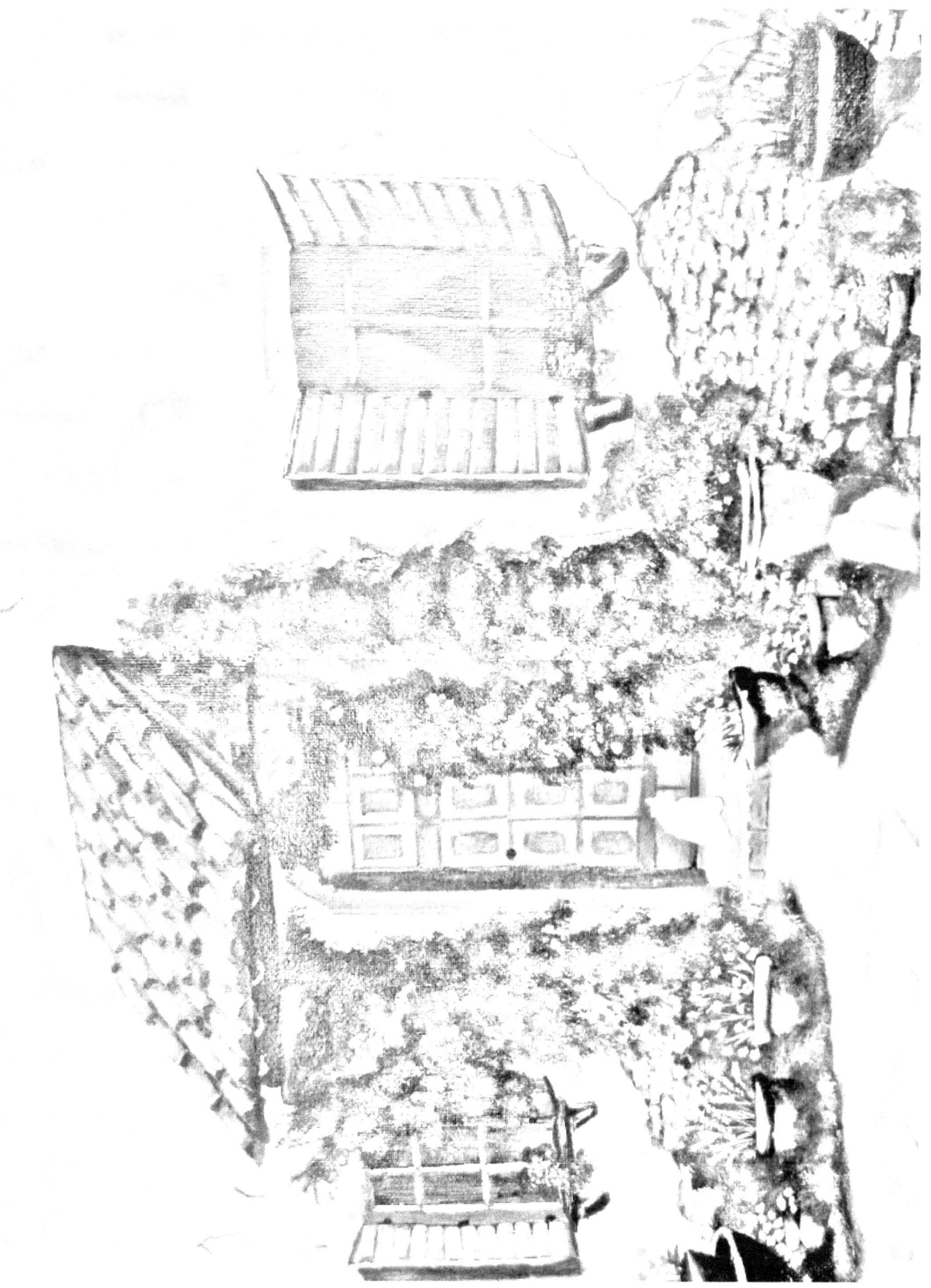

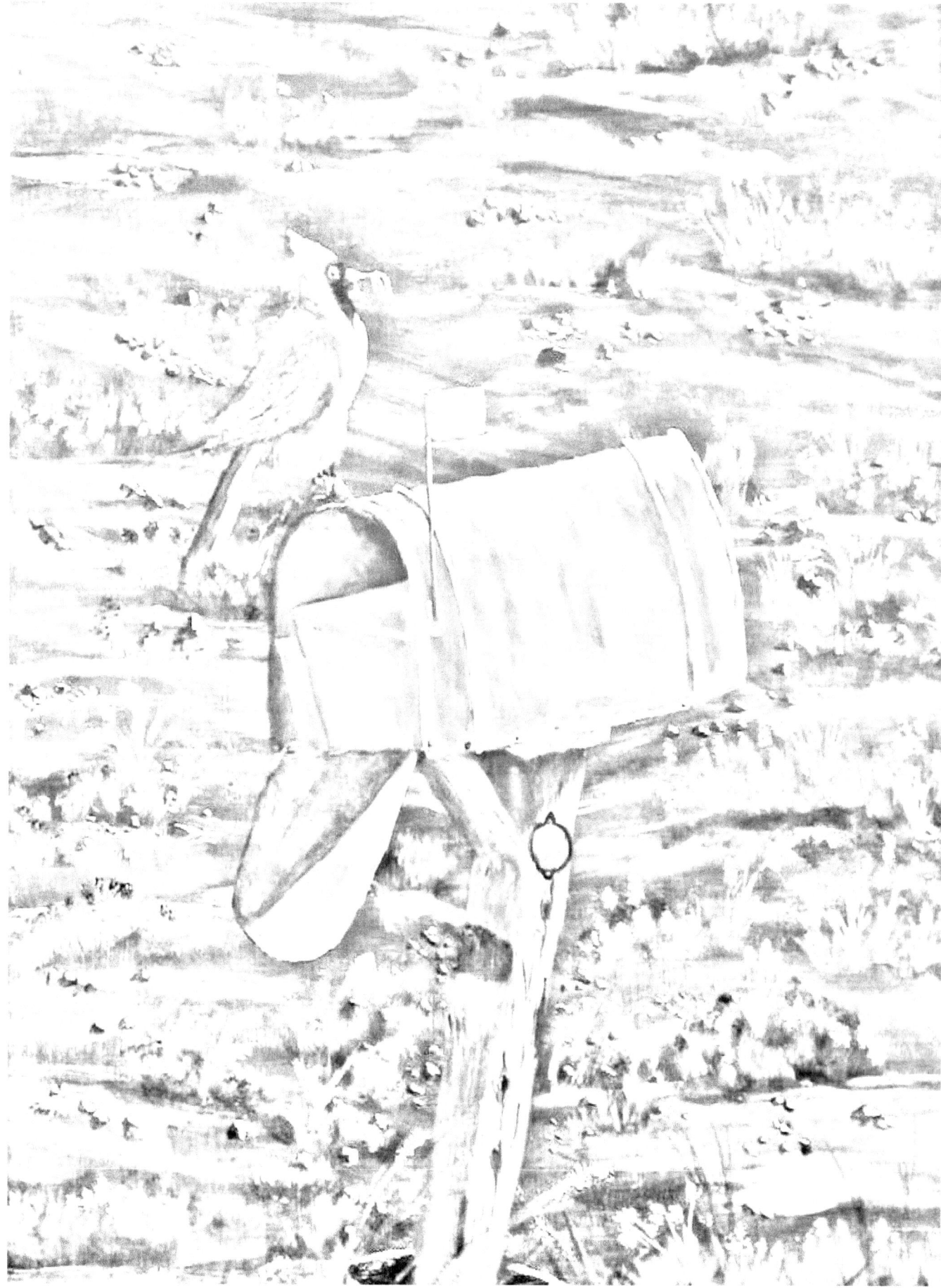

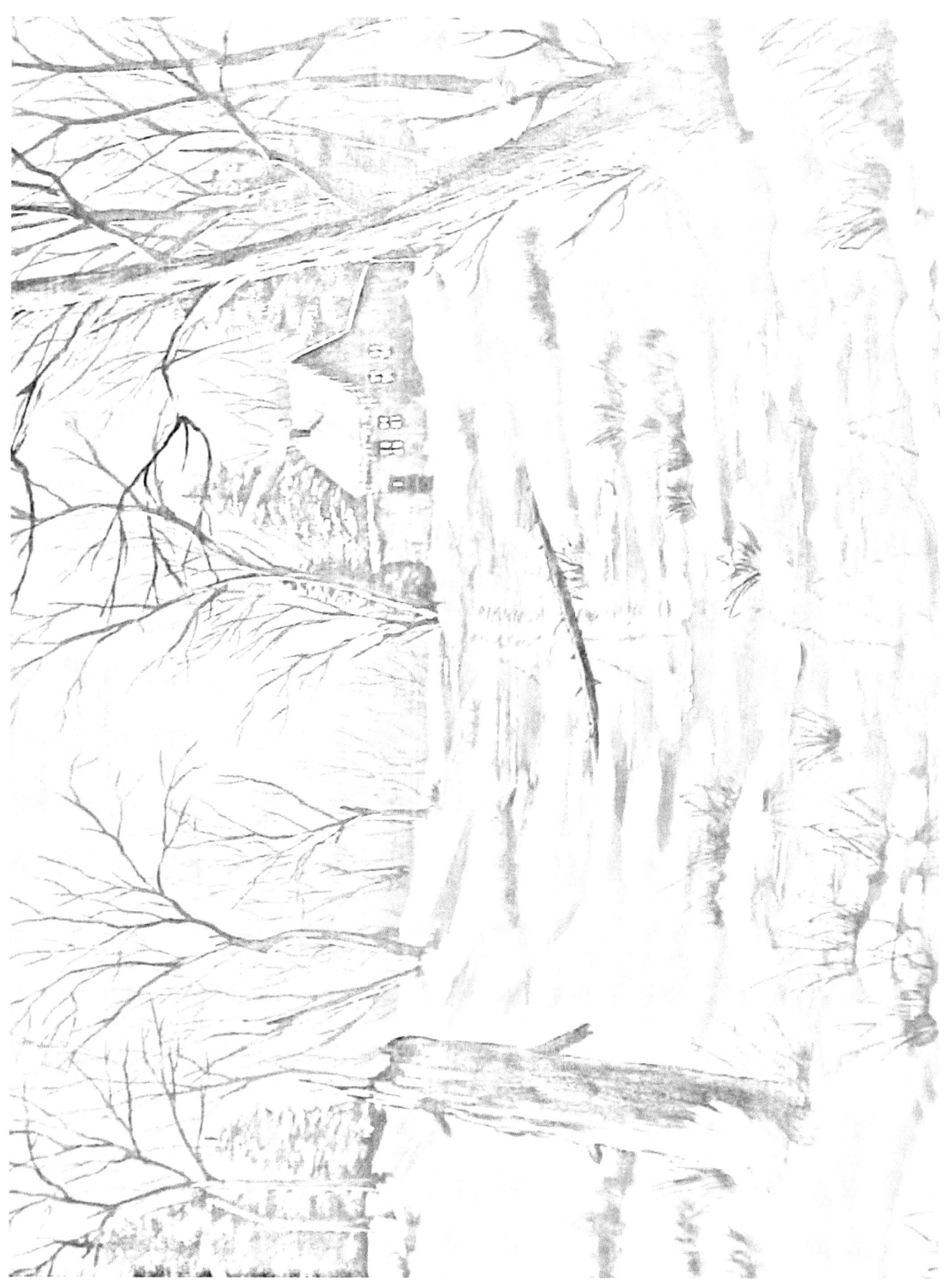

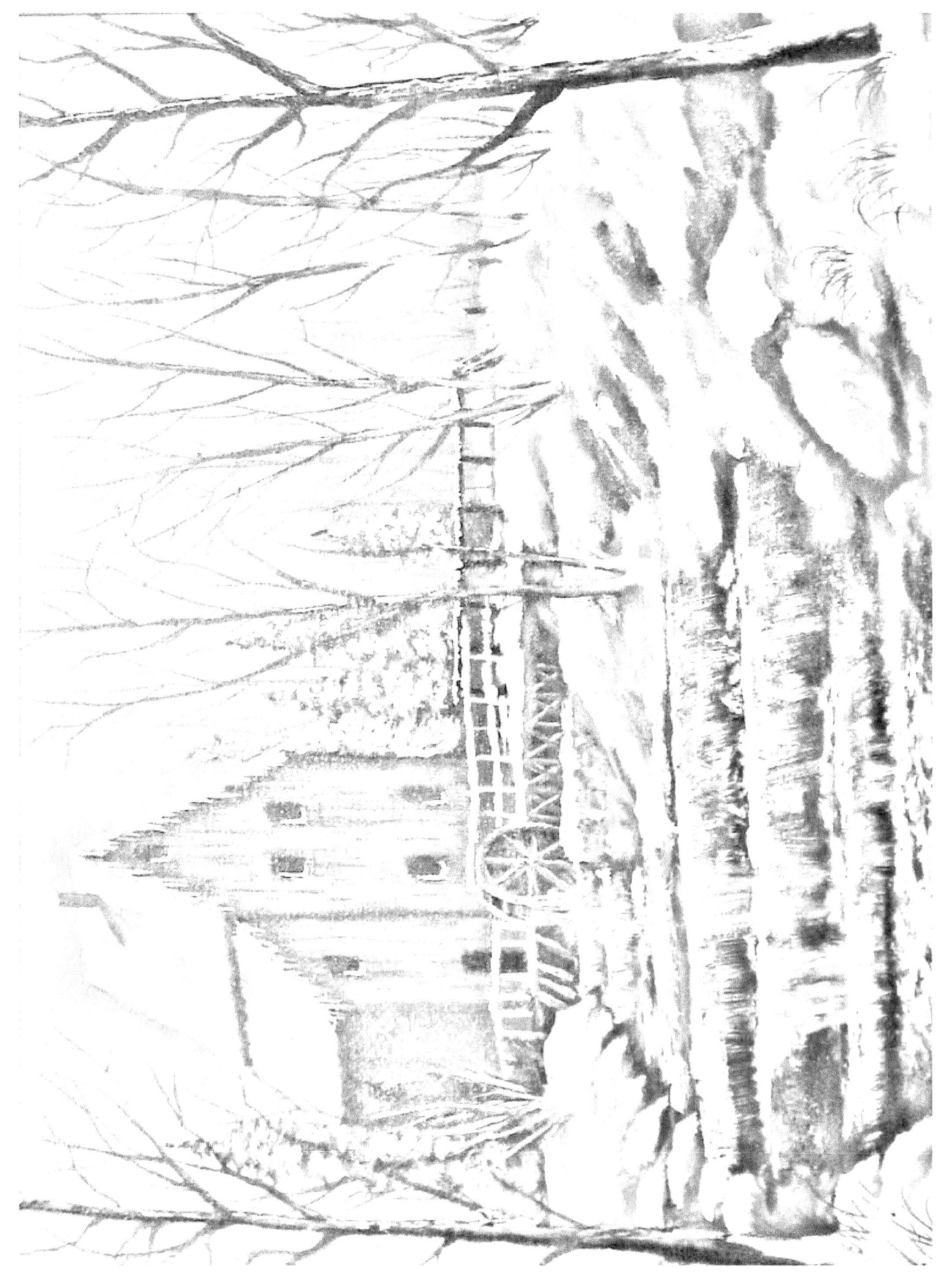

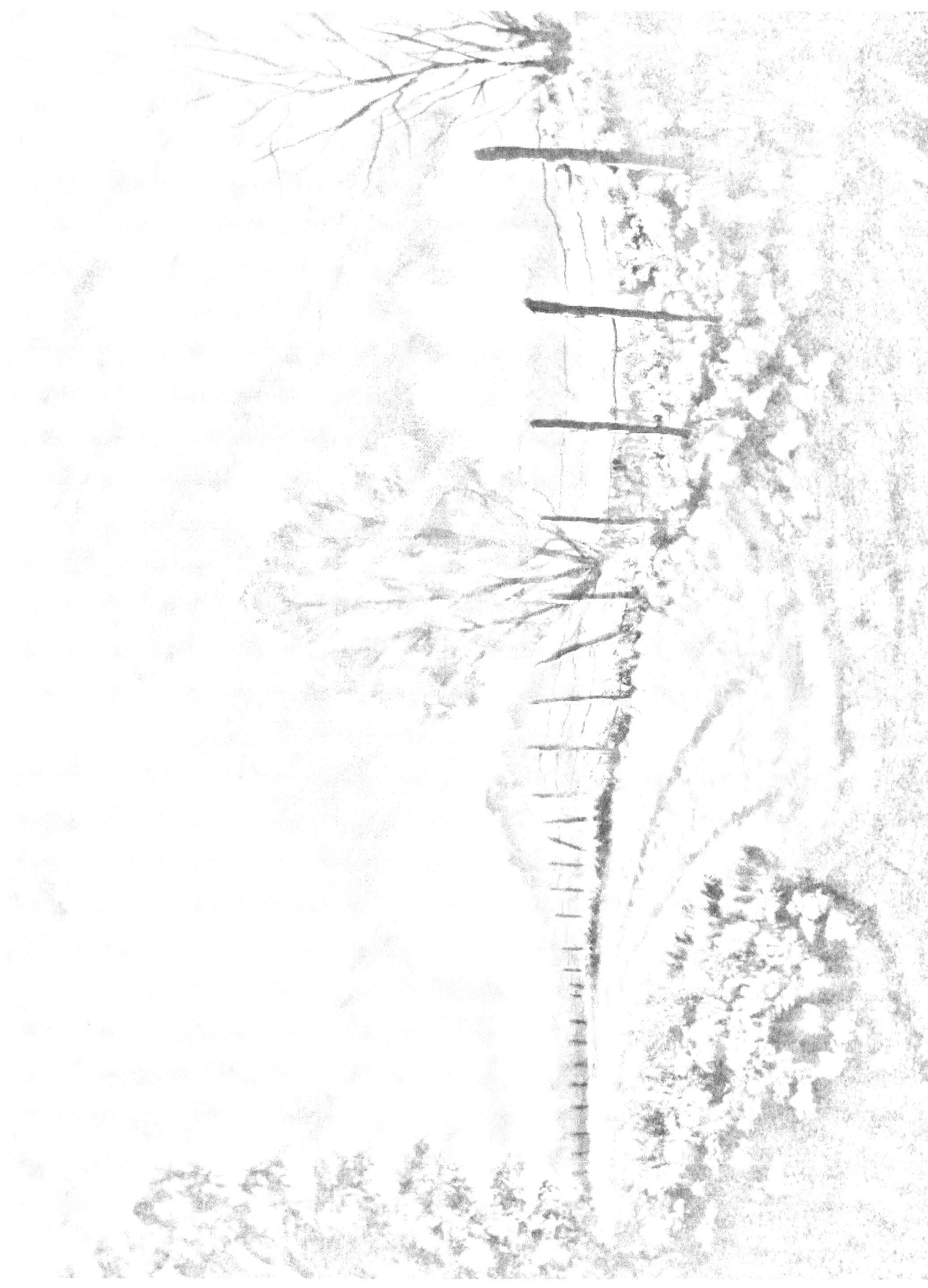

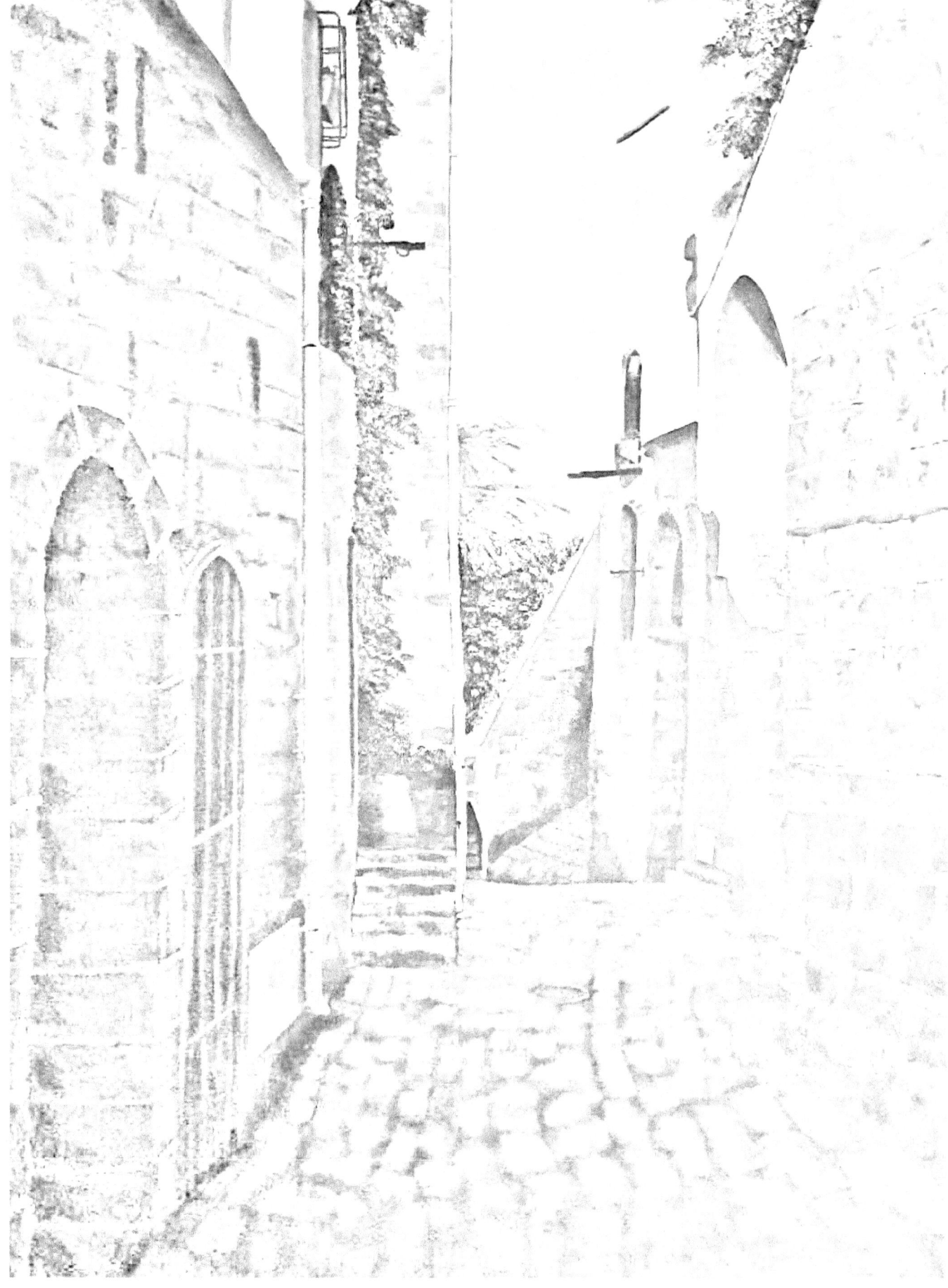

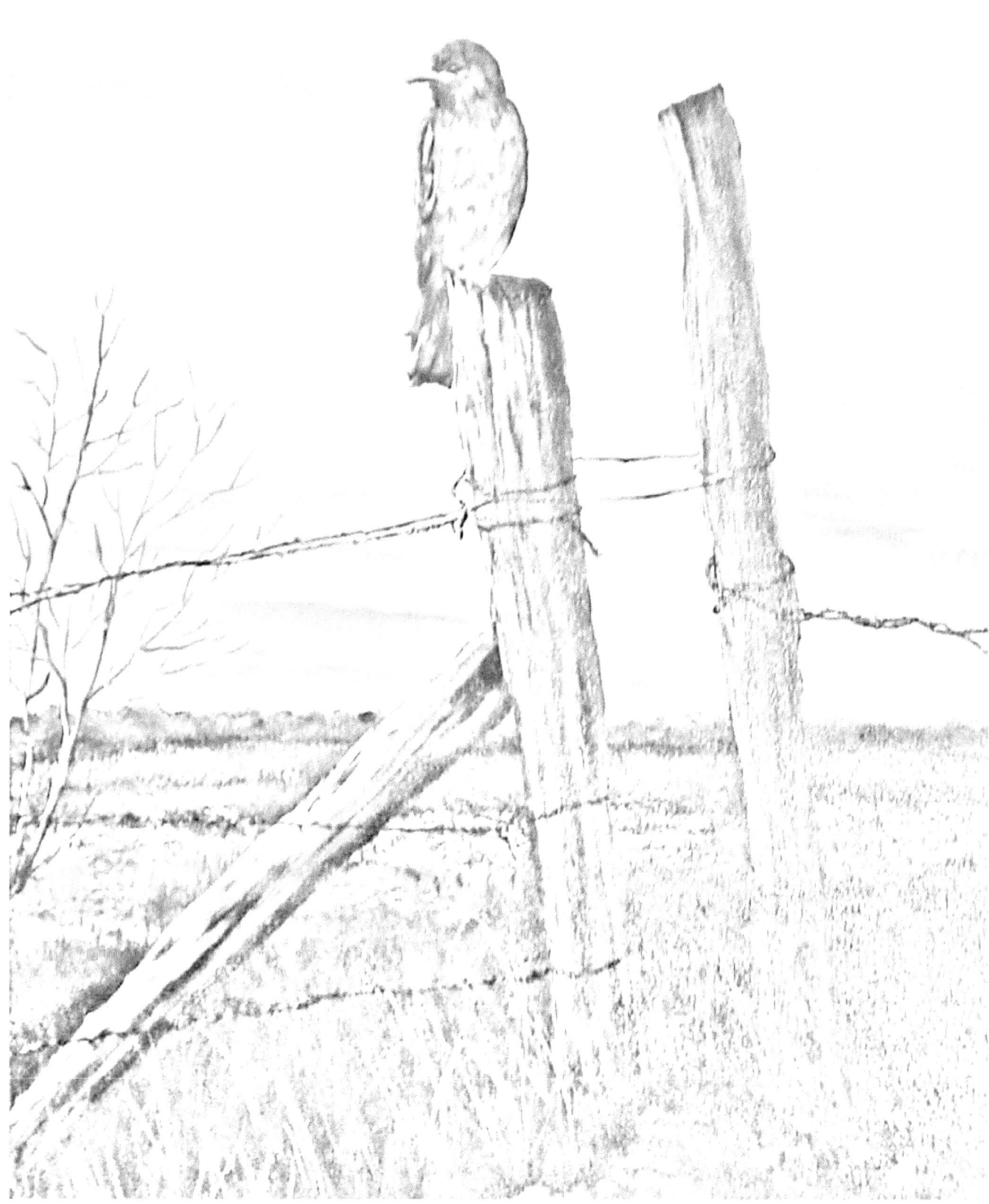

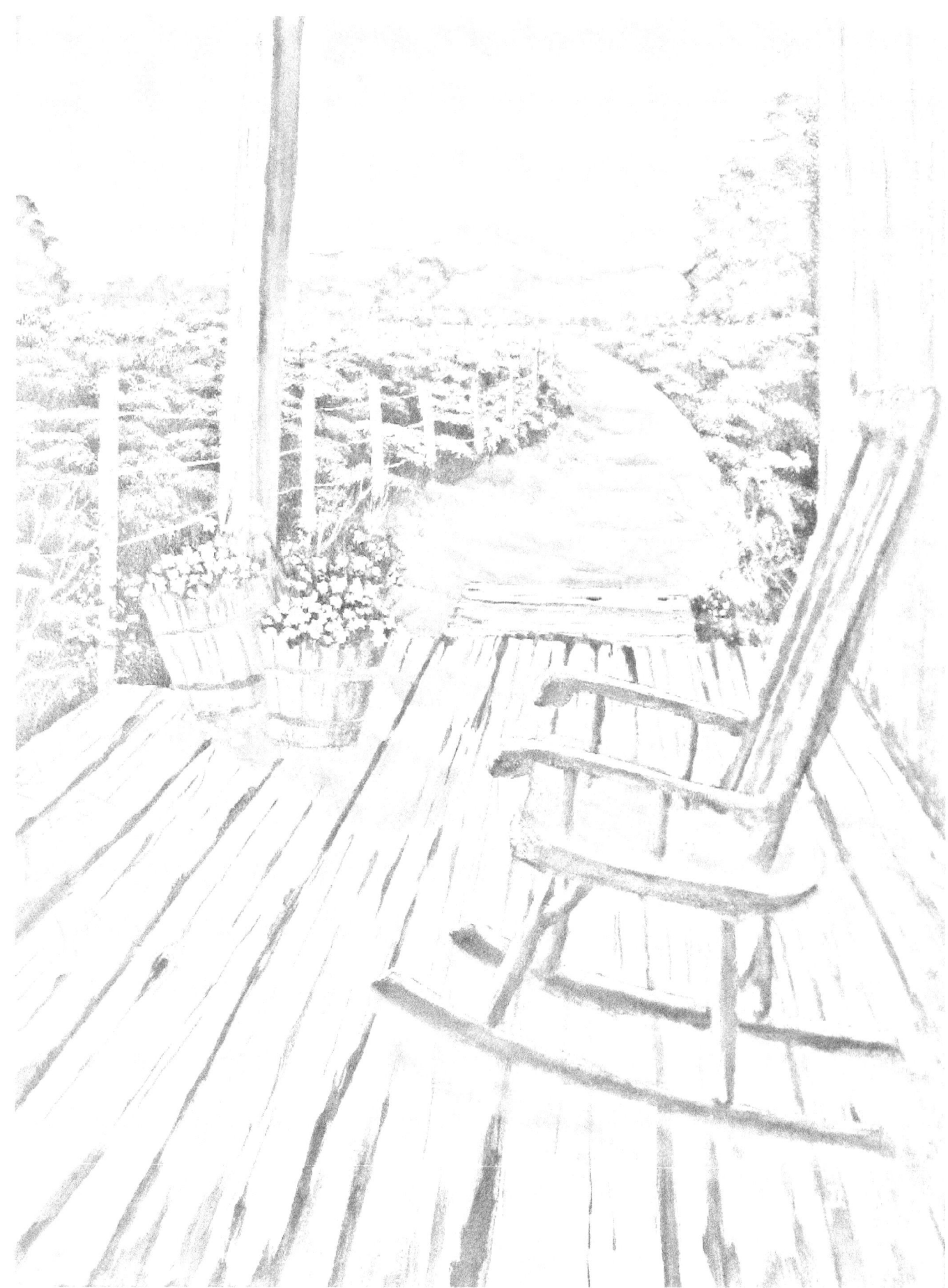

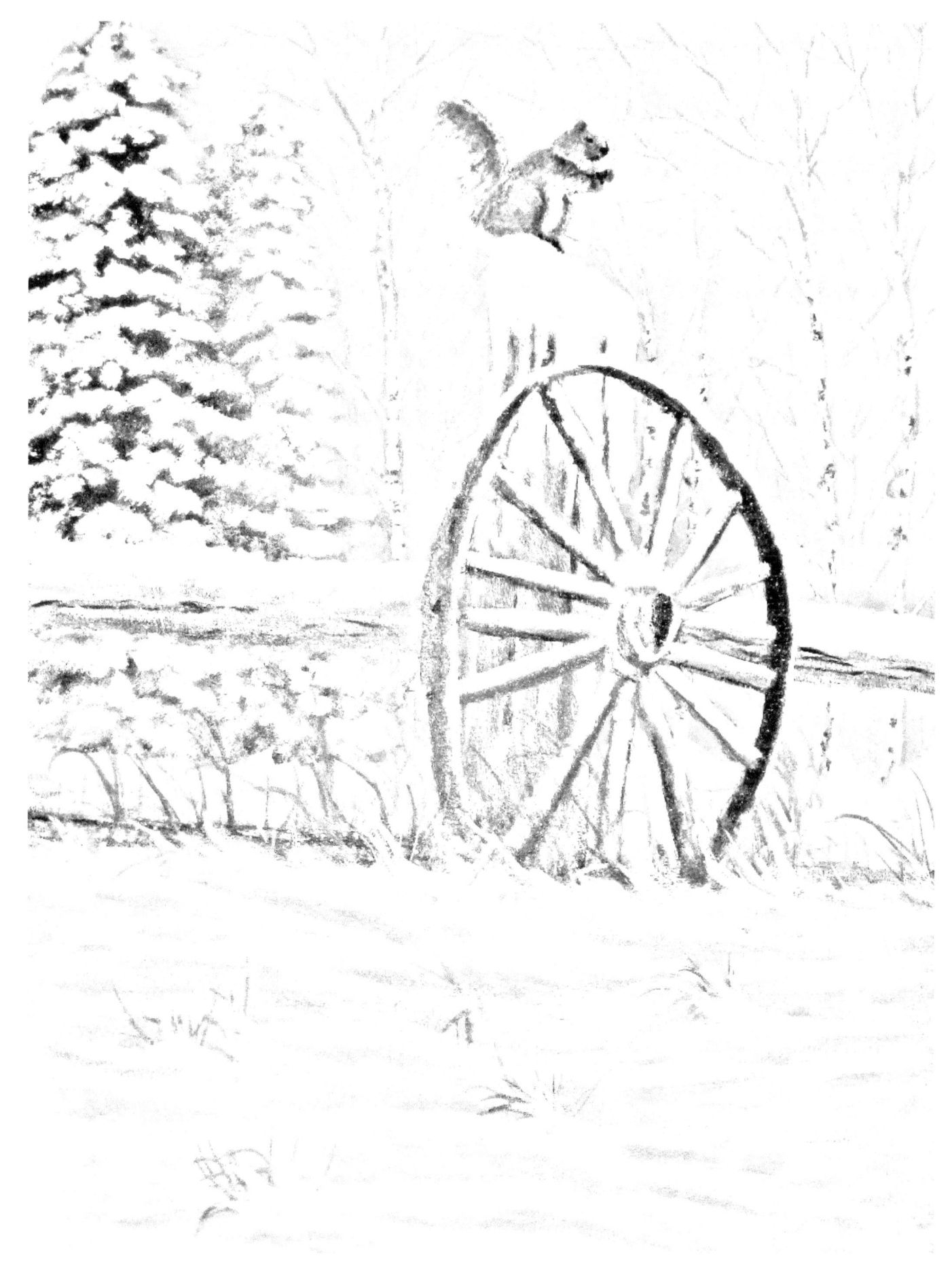

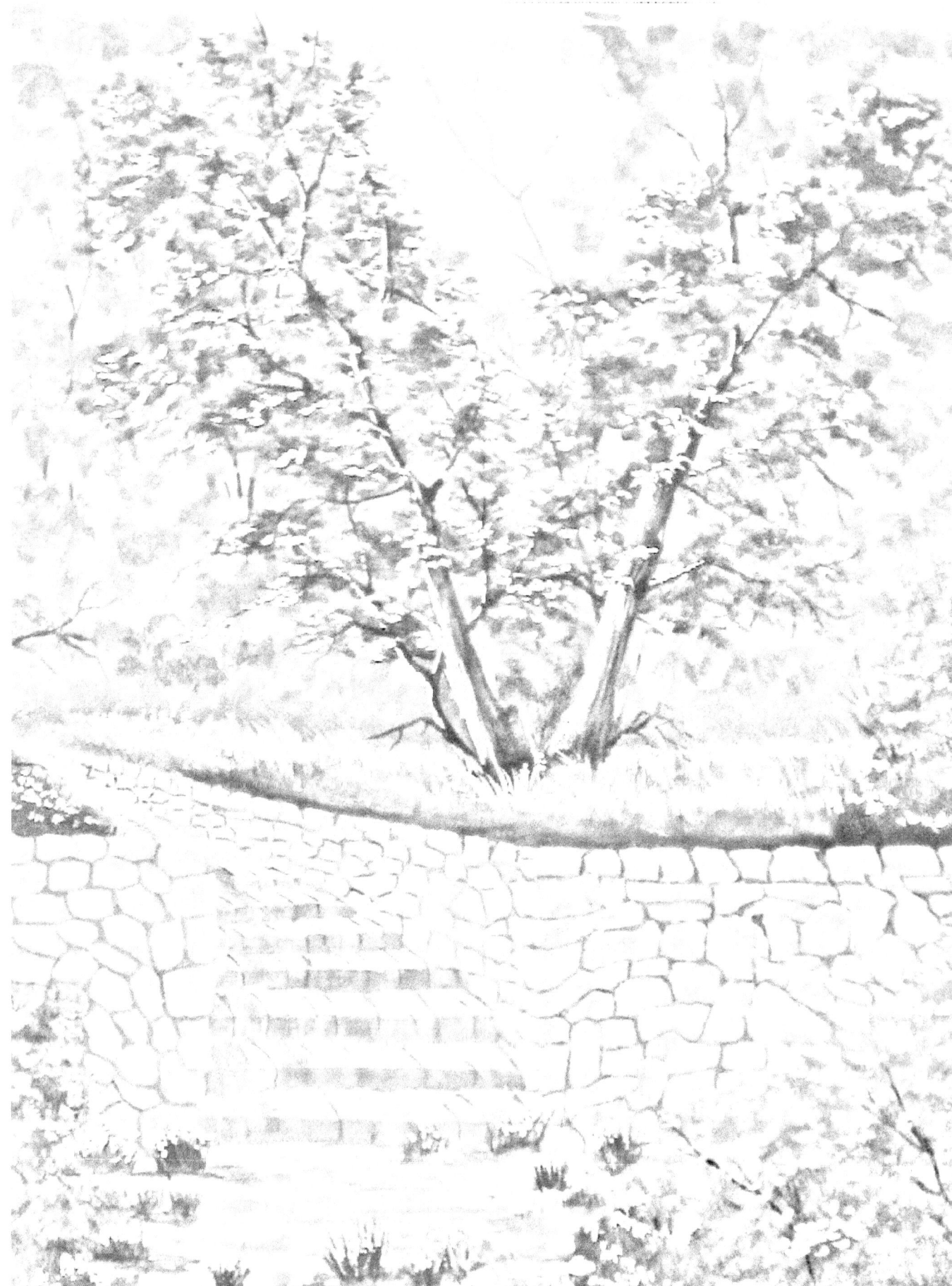

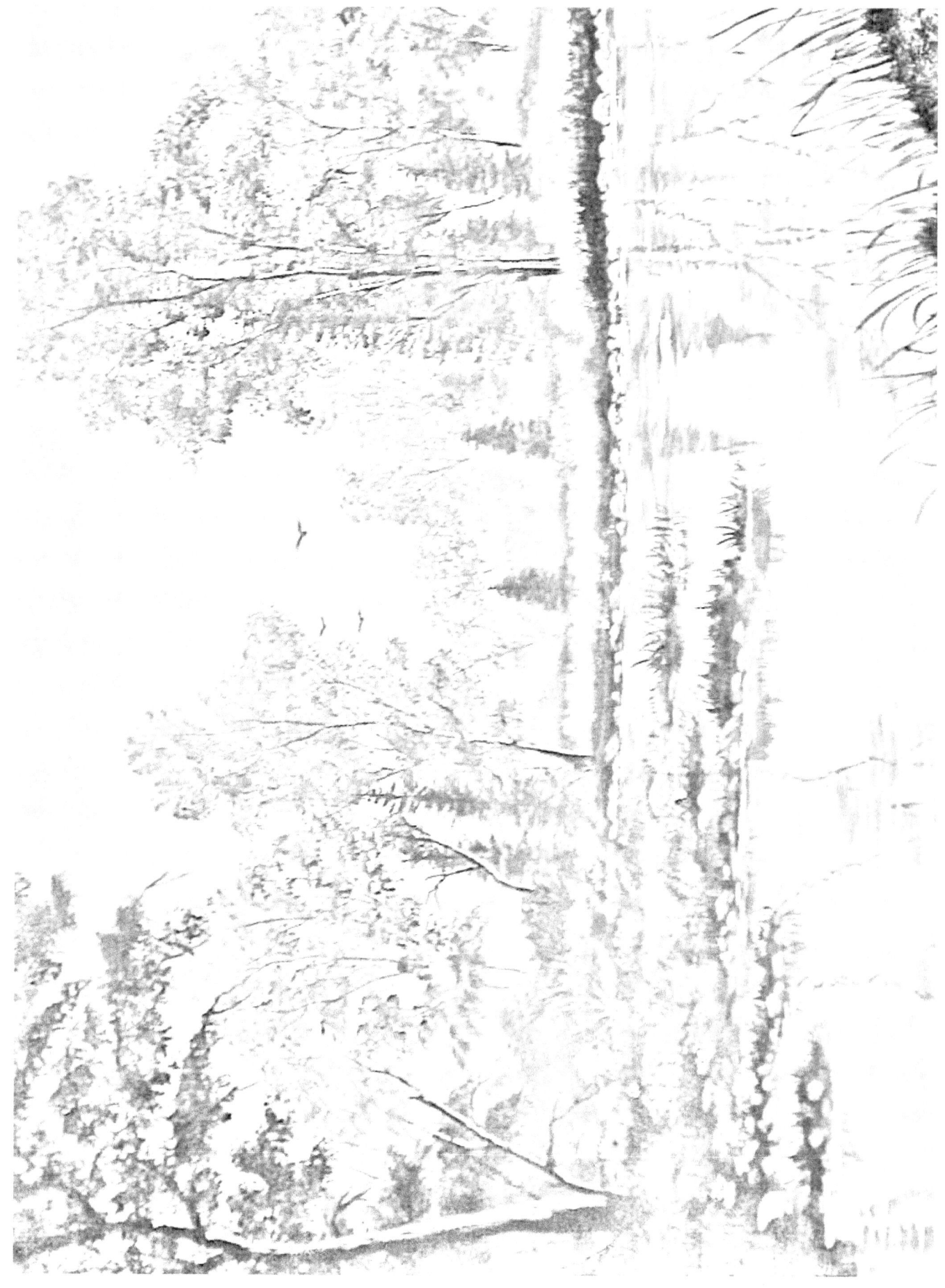

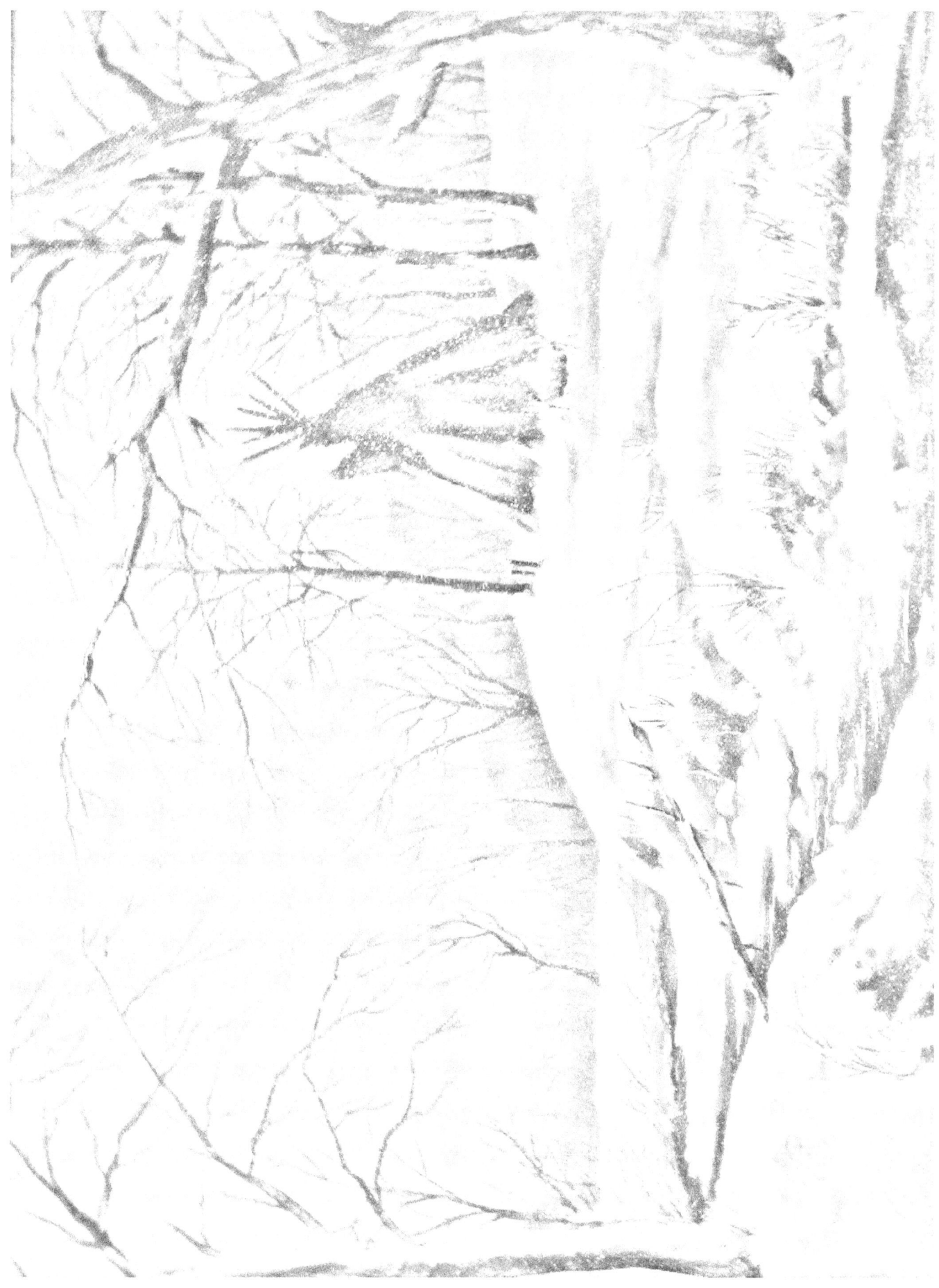

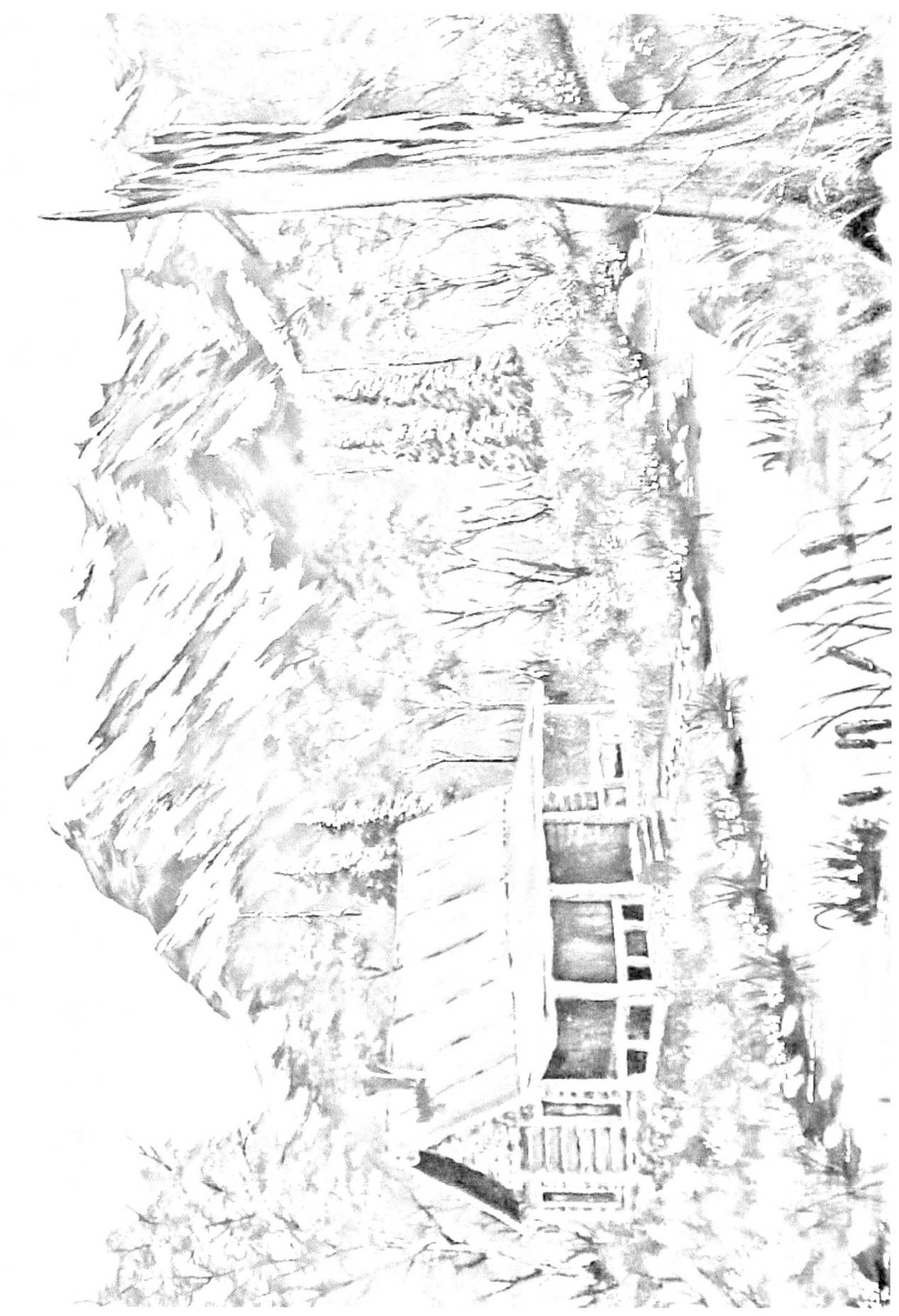

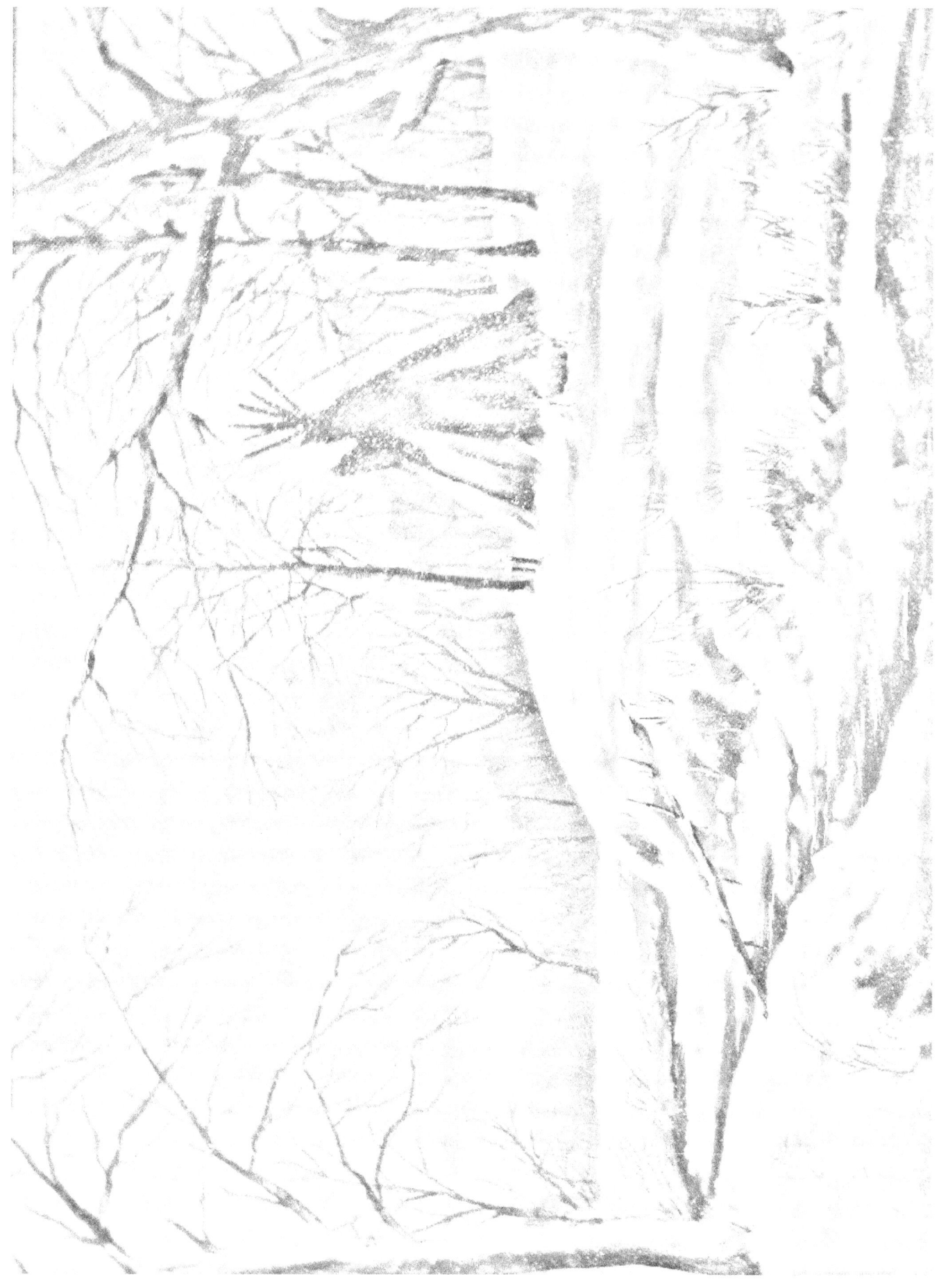

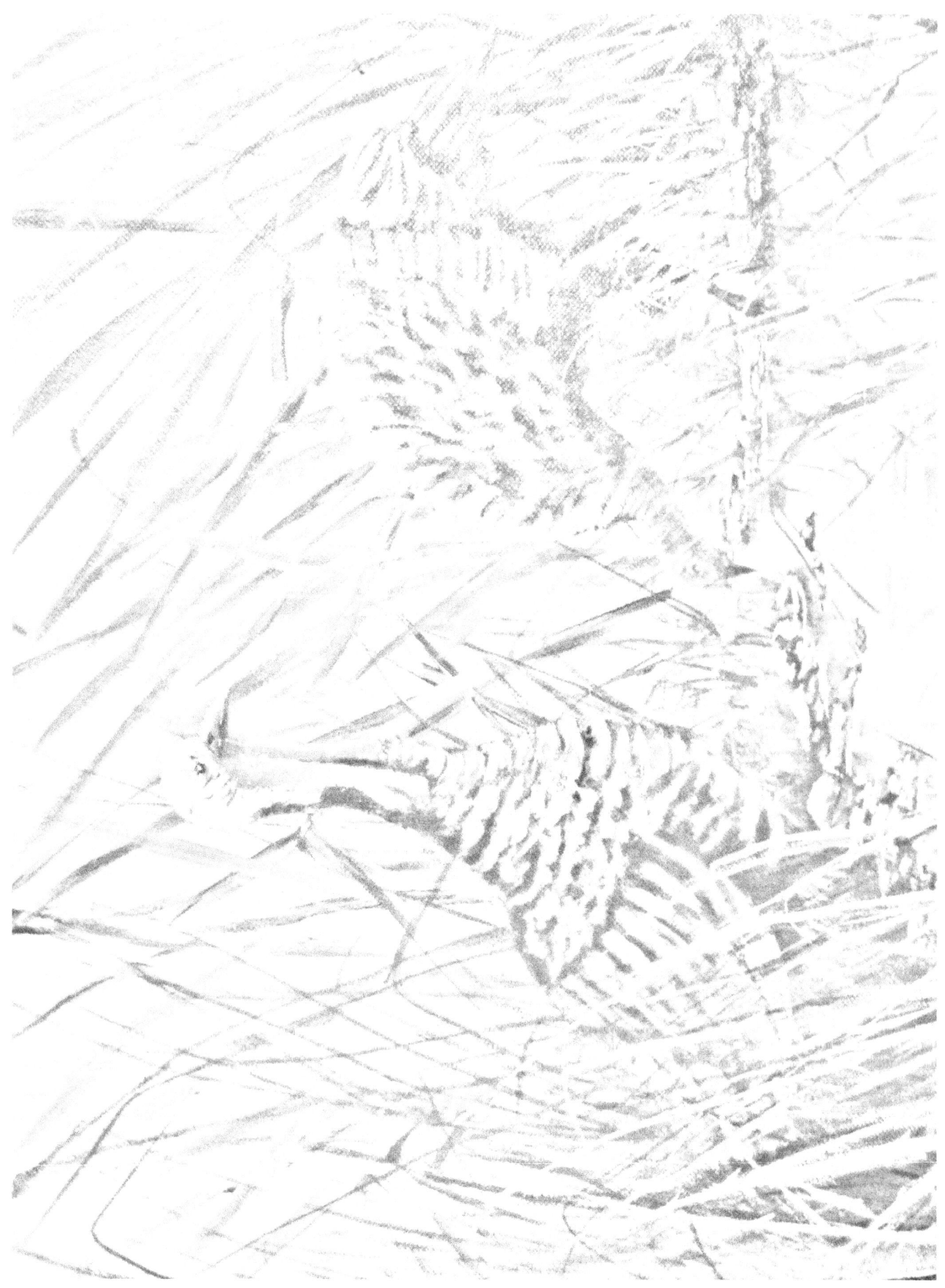

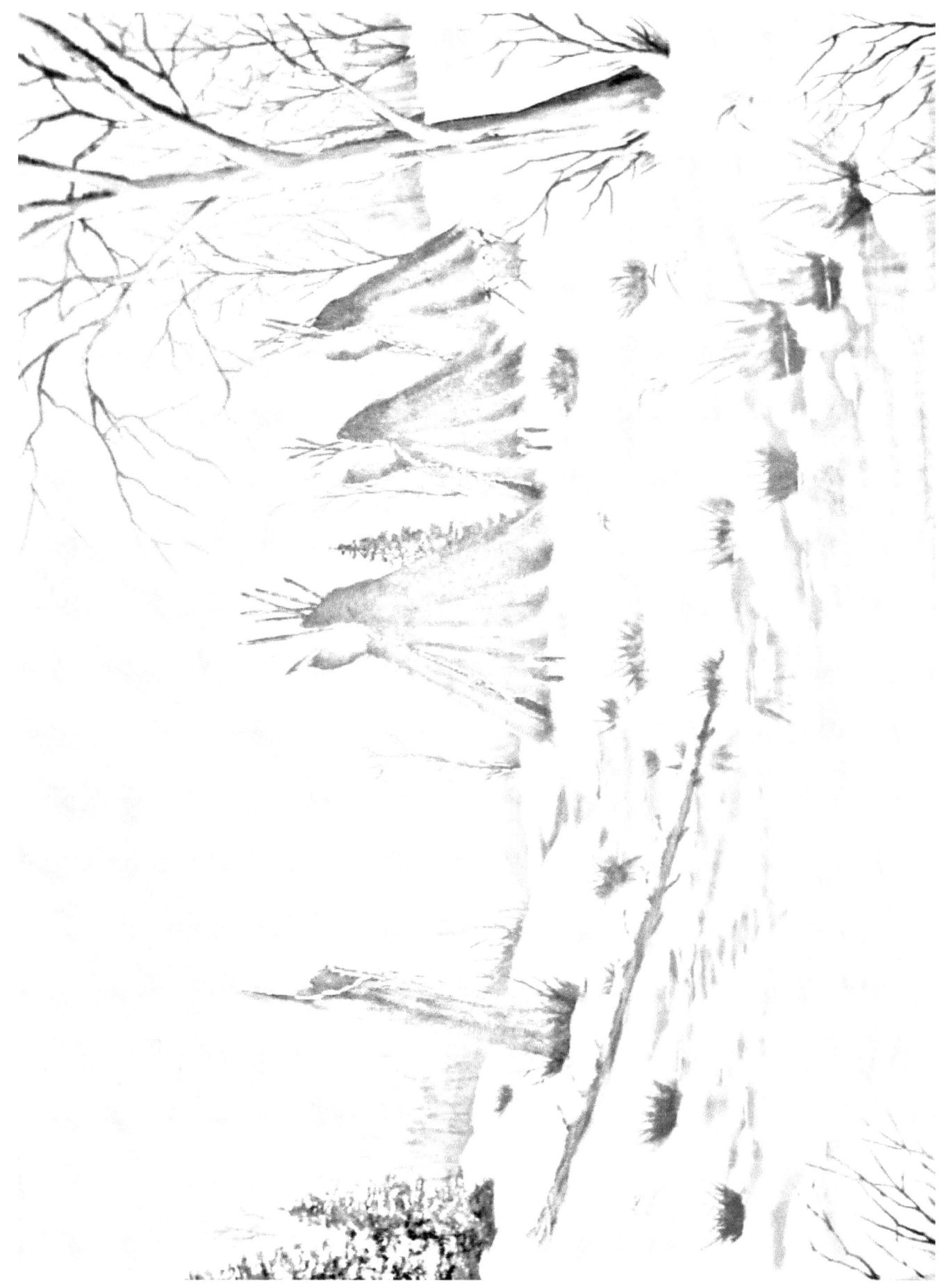

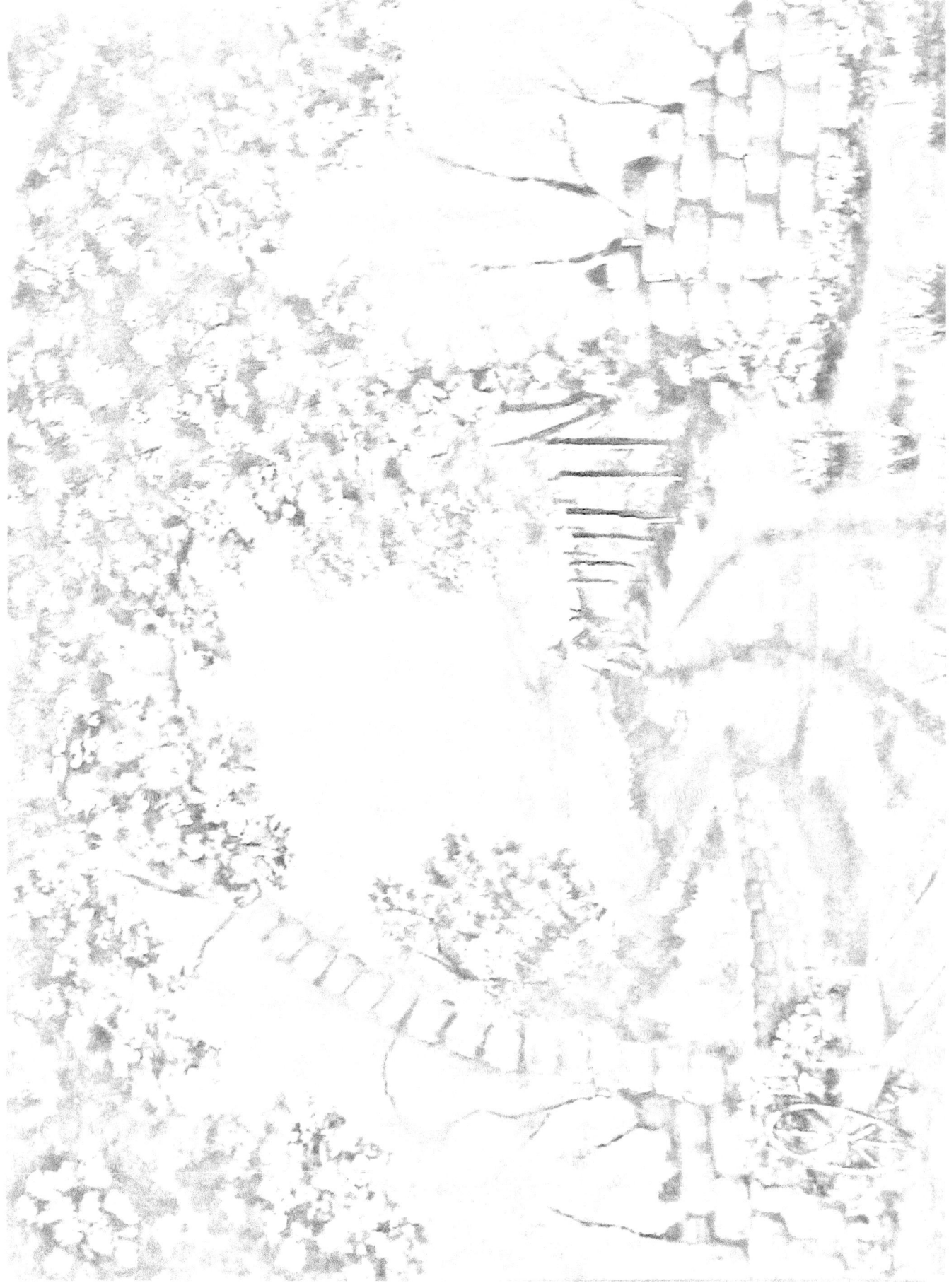

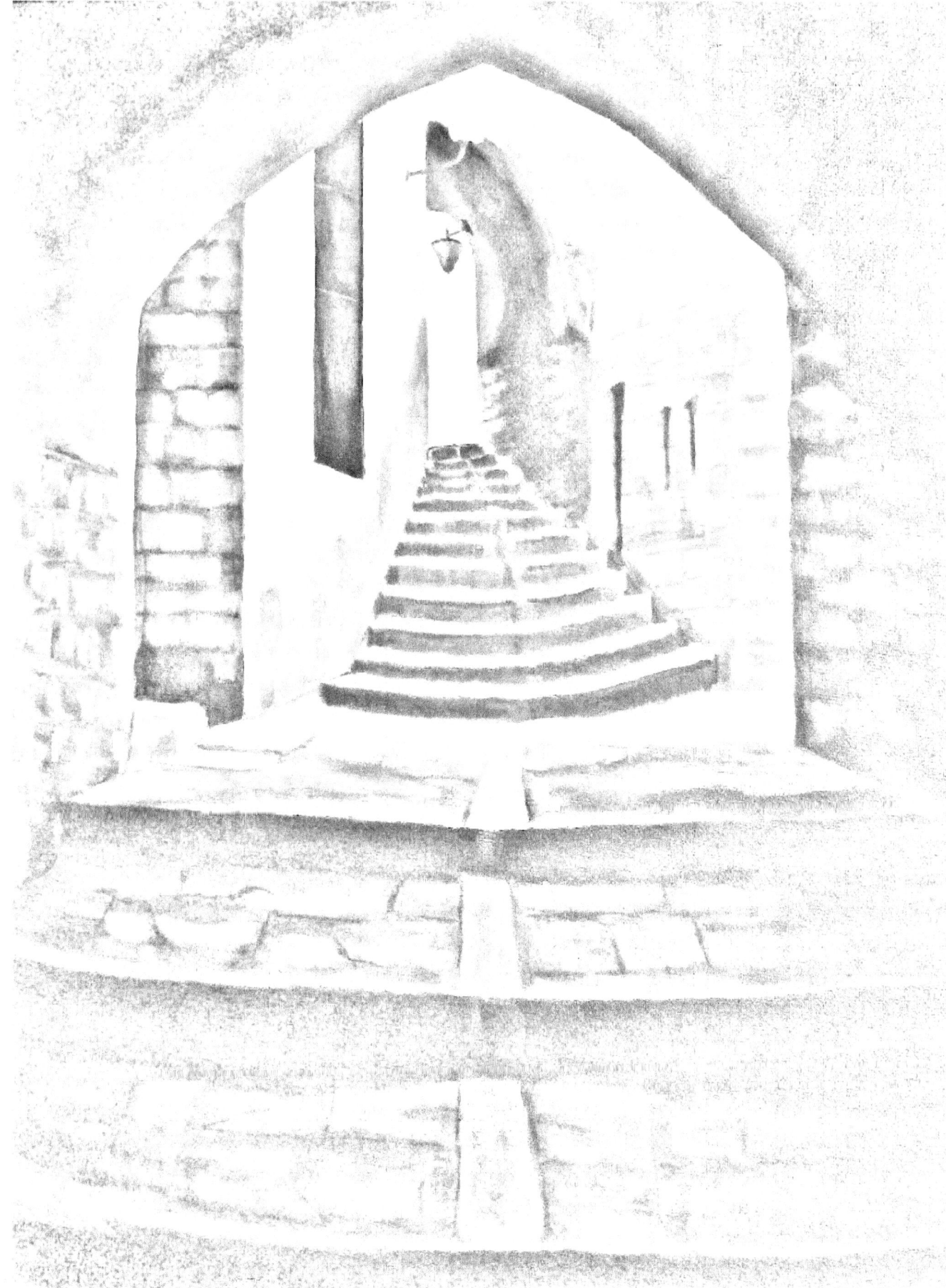

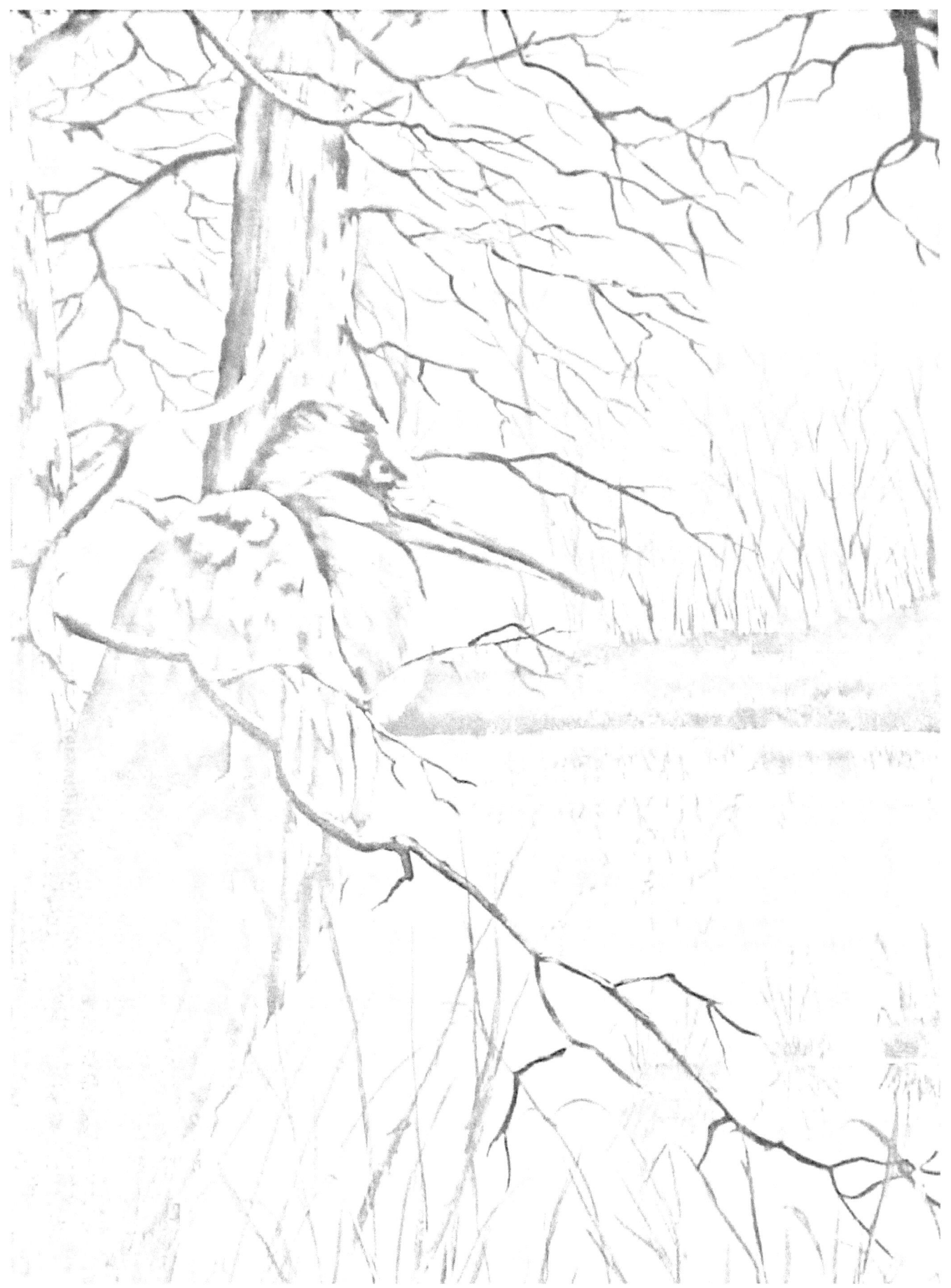

I hope you have enjoyed volume 1 of Landscape & Outdoors Coloring book! Look for Volume 2 coming soon with even more beautiful pictures to color.

Don La Due